GRAMMAR
AND BEYOND

**Teacher Support Resource Book
with CD-ROM**

Paul Carne

Elizabeth Henly

Jenni Currie Santamaria

Jane Sturtevant

2

CAMBRIDGE
UNIVERSITY PRESS

CAMBRIDGE UNIVERSITY PRESS
Cambridge, New York, Melbourne, Madrid, Cape Town,
Singapore, São Paulo, Delhi, Tokyo, Mexico City

Cambridge University Press
32 Avenue of the Americas, New York, NY 10013-2473, USA

www.cambridge.org
Information on this title: www.cambridge.org/9781107676534

First published 2012

Printed in the United States of America

A catalog record for this publication is available from the British Library.

ISBN 978-0-521-14296-0 Student's Book 2
ISBN 978-0-521-14310-3 Student's Book 2A
ISBN 978-0-521-14312-7 Student's Book 2B
ISBN 978-0-521-27991-8 Workbook 2
ISBN 978-0-521-27992-5 Workbook 2A
ISBN 978-0-521-27993-2 Workbook 2B
ISBN 978-1-107-67653-4 Teacher Support Resource 2
ISBN 978-0-521-14335-6 Class Audio 2
ISBN 978-1-139-06186-5 Writing Skills Interactive 2

Cambridge University Press has no responsibility for the persistence or
accuracy of URLs for external or third-party Internet Web sites referred to in
this publication and does not guarantee that any content on such Web sites is,
or will remain, accurate or appropriate. Information regarding prices, travel
timetables, and other factual information given in this work is correct at
the time of first printing, but Cambridge University Press does not guarantee
the accuracy of such information thereafter.

It is normally necessary for written permission for copying to be obtained in
advance from a publisher. The tests on the CD-ROM at the back of this book
are designed to be copied and distributed in class. The normal requirements are
waived here, and it is not necessary to write to Cambridge University Press for
permission for an individual teacher to make copies for use within his or her own
classroom. Only those pages which carry the wording "©Cambridge University
Press" may be copied.

Layout services: TSI Graphics

Contents

Introduction

Grammar and Beyond is a four-level grammar series for beginning- to advanced-level students of North American English. The series focuses on the most commonly used grammar structures and their most common meanings and uses. It features a special emphasis on the application of these structures in academic writing. There is also a focus on authentic language use in communicative contexts.

A Unique Approach

Research Based

The grammar presented is strongly informed by the *Cambridge International Corpus.* This corpus was created from the research and analysis of over one billion words of authentic written and spoken language data gathered from college lectures, textbooks, academic essays, high school classrooms, and conversations between instructors and students. By using the *Cambridge International Corpus,* the series contributors were able to:

- Present grammar rules that reflect actual North American English
- Describe differences between the grammar of written and spoken English
- Focus more attention on the structures that are commonly used, and less on those that are rarely used, in both written and spoken language

Academic Writing Skills

The structure of *Grammar and Beyond* is designed to help students make the transition from simply understanding grammar structures to actually using them accurately in writing.

Error Avoidance

Each Student's Book unit features an *Avoid Common Mistakes* section that develops awareness of the most common mistakes made by English language learners and provides practice in detecting and correcting these errors. The mistakes highlighted in this section are drawn from the *Cambridge Learner Corpus,* a database of over 135,000 essays written by nonnative speakers of English.

Vocabulary

Every unit in *Grammar and Beyond* includes words from the Academic Word List (AWL), a research-based list of words and word families that appear with high frequency in academic texts. These words are introduced in the opening text of the unit, recycled in the charts and exercises, and used to support the theme throughout the unit. The same vocabulary is reviewed and practiced in the corresponding unit of *Writing Skills Interactive*.

Instructional Resources

Teacher Support Resource Book with CD-ROM

In addition to an answer key and audio script for the Student's Book, this book contains general teaching suggestions for applying any of the structures taught in the Student's Book to all four major skill areas.

The CD-ROM in the back of this book includes:

PowerPoint Presentations

Thirty-two animated presentations offer unit-specific grammar lessons for classroom use. Their purpose is to provide engaging visual aids to help clarify complex grammatical concepts while encouraging a high level of student involvement.

Unit Tests

Each of the 32 ready-made unit tests consists of two parts. Part I tests the grammar points in the order presented in the unit. Part II offers a more challenging blend of the grammar. Each unit test is easy to score on a scale of 100 points by following the guidelines included in the answer key, also found on the CD-ROM. Each unit test is available in two formats: as a PDF (portable document format) and as a Microsoft Word document. The Word documents are provided for those instructors who wish to customize the tests.

Online Unit-by-Unit Teaching Suggestions

The Unit-by-Unit Teaching Suggestions (downloadable at www.cambridge.org/grammarandbeyond) include unit-specific suggestions for expansion as well as the following suggestions.

- **Tech It Up:** Tips for using technology to practice the target grammar
- **Beware:** Troubleshooting ideas for common problems with the target grammar
- **Register:** Suggestions for addressing formality and native language usage as it applies to the target grammar
- **Always an Exception:** Notes about exceptions to rules
- **Game Time:** Ideas for games and other group activities that provide further practice

Student Book Ancillaries

The following resources enhance the learning experience.

Class Audio CD

The Class Audio CD provides all Student's Book listening material for in-class use.

Workbook

The Workbook provides additional practice of the grammar presented in the Student's Book. All exercises can be assigned for homework or can be completed in class.

Writing Skills Interactive

Writing Skills Interactive is an online interactive program that provides instruction and practice in key skills crucial for academic writing (writing effective topic sentences, avoiding sentence fragments, distinguishing between fact and opinion, etc.). The units of *Writing Skills Interactive* correspond to and build on Student's Book units through shared vocabulary and themes.

Program Highlights

- Each unit includes an animated presentation that provides interactive, dynamic instruction in the writing skill.
- Academic and content vocabulary introduced in the corresponding Student's Book unit are recycled and practiced through the use of additional theme-based contexts.
- The presentation in each *Writing Skills Interactive* unit is followed by focused practice with immediate feedback.
- The program allows students to work at their own pace and review instructional presentations as needed. It is ideal for individual learning and practice, although it can also be used successfully in the classroom or computer lab.

General Teaching Suggestions

This guide provides a variety of strategies to use with recurring unit sections and exercise types in the *Grammar and Beyond* Student's Book. For expansion activities, technology-related activities, and ideas developed for individual units, refer to the Unit-by-Unit Teaching Suggestions, downloadable free of charge at www.cambridge.org/grammarandbeyond.

Student Self-Assessment

Refer to the Unit-by-Unit Teaching Suggestions (downloadable at www.cambridge.org/grammarandbeyond) for the list of objectives for the unit. Write them on the board, and ask students to copy them. Then have students do a brief self-assessment on each objective by choosing from the three options:

> *Self-Assessment, Unit* _____
> *Objective* _____
>
> ☐ 1. *I know a lot about this and can use it easily.*
> ☐ 2. *I know something about this but need more practice.*
> ☐ 3. *I don't know very much about this.*

Revisit the statements when you have completed the unit so that students can assess their progress.

Pre-unit Assessment Strategies

Prior Knowledge of Target Grammar

Before you begin the unit, you will probably want to do a brief assessment of students' prior knowledge of the grammar point. A grammar pre-assessment helps you determine whether students understand the meaning of the structure, whether they can produce the form, and whether they are able to integrate it into their writing and spontaneous speech. Here are some ways to help you obtain this information quickly.

■ To determine whether students understand the target language, write several sentences on the board using the structure (for example, *John has lived in Washington for 10 years.*). Ask questions to elicit information about the meaning of the sentences. (*Does John live in Washington now? Did John live in Washington five years ago?*)

■ To determine whether students can describe and reproduce the form, ask them to identify, for example, the part of speech, verb forms, or auxiliaries of the target structure. (*What is the verb in this sentence? What tense is it? How do you form the present perfect?*) Write two or three fill-in-the-blank sentences on the board, and ask students to complete them with the target structure.

(*There _____ several earthquakes this year. The reporter _____ a lot of questions.*) Ask students to complete the sentences. Walk around and spot-check their answers to assess students' familiarity with the structure.

■ If most of the students are able to do the sentence completion, check their ability to use the grammar in a less controlled activity by asking a question to elicit the target language. (*What has the weather been like lately?*) Have them respond in writing with one or two complete sentences. Collect their work so you can assess the class as a whole (and not just a few students). You can also use this information for pairing and grouping later. Note the grammar used in students' responses, but do not correct or begin teaching the structure explicitly at this point. Tell students that they will be learning the structure in the upcoming unit. You may want to save your notes and write the students' sentences on the board when you have completed the unit so they can identify their errors and see solid evidence of their progress.

■ If many of your students are able to produce the structure correctly in response to your question eliciting the target language, you can move more quickly through the controlled practice in the unit and spend more time focusing on the more open-ended writing and speaking activities. Tell students that although they may be familiar with the structure, it is your objective to help them put the grammar to use in their speaking and writing.

General Strategies for Unit Sections

Grammar in the Real World

This section introduces the target structure(s) in an authentic context, such as a website or short article. A *Notice* activity draws students' attention to the form or function of the target structures in the text. The following strategies can be used with this section. See the Unit-by-Unit Teaching Suggestions, downloadable free of charge at www.cambridge.org/grammarandbeyond.com, for text-specific notes and vocabulary lists.

Pre-reading/Warm Up

■ Direct students' attention to the picture. Ask them to describe it, or ask specific questions about it (*What's happening? Who/Where do you think the person is?*). Ask students about their personal experiences or opinions related to the picture. (*Have you ever done this? How do you feel when this happens to you? What do you think about this?*)

■ Ask students to read the title of the text and make one or two predictions about the content. Write students' predictions on the board. After they have read the text, compare their predictions to what they have read.

Pre-teaching the Vocabulary

Before students read, look through the text and make a list of words they may not know. Alternatively, use the word list, with Academic Word List (AWL) vocabulary labeled, found in the Unit-by-Unit Teaching Suggestions, downloadable free of charge at www.cambridge.org/grammarandbeyond. Try one or both of these techniques:

- List the words on the board, and ask students to discuss their meanings in small groups. Ask students for definitions. Make a note of words that students find difficult.

- List the words on one side of the board and their corresponding definitions on the other side (in a different order), and ask students to match them. Have students write down any words that are new. To save time in class, write the words and definitions on separate cards in advance and post them where students can see them.

Glossed Vocabulary

Paying attention to text signals, like footnotes, is an important academic skill. Therefore, you may not want to include the glossed vocabulary among the words you pre-teach. Instead, draw students' attention to the footnote numbers, and encourage them to watch for them while reading. Provide any clarification students need about the glossed words.

Comprehension Check

- To accommodate a variety of levels, have students complete the *Comprehension Check* individually. Write an additional comprehension question or a related question on the board for early finishers to answer.

- If you think the activity is too challenging for some of your students, have them compare their answers with a partner before you review the answers as a class. This gives students a low-stress way of checking their work. Consider pairing students of different levels based on your pre-assessment.

Notice

- The *Notice* activity guides students to find the target language in the text. Explain that scanning quickly for specific words is often an effective way to find the target language (for example, suggest that they look for the words *have* or *has* in a unit on the present perfect). To get them started, have students look at item 1 and tell you which word they should scan for.

- In some cases, you may want students to try to give answers before they look for them in the text. Ask students to share their answers. Then have students scan the article to find the correct answers.

- Have students do the first part of the activity (finding the target language) individually. Then have them work in pairs to discuss the question or complete the final part of the activity.

Grammar Presentations

Each unit includes at least one of these sections, which provide chart-based presentations of the target grammar. They address both structure and usage, and offer examples that reflect the unit theme. The section may also include a *Data from the Real World* box, providing real-world usage notes based on extensive corpus research.

Overview Box

Read the information in the overview box that introduces each set of grammar charts. Explain that this box highlights a key feature of the grammar point. Ask students what the connection is between the introductory information and the example sentences.

Grammar Charts

Teach students the value of the charts as a reference tool. When they make mistakes, ask them to look at the relevant chart to self-correct. If possible, keep a copy of the current chart(s) visible in the classroom for easy reference. Following are some ways to present the charts in class.

Structure Charts

Some charts, like the one that follows, break down the structure of the target language, with target language in bold. Here are some possibilities for teaching structure charts.

Time Context	*Wh-* Word	*Would*	Subject	Base Form of Verb	
In the past,	**how** **where**	**would**	I you he/she/it we they	**heat**	the water?

- Have students start the lesson with books closed. Write one of the examples from the chart on the board. Ask questions to check students' understanding of the grammar. (*What's the subject? What's the verb?*) Write labels above the example so that you are recreating the chart headings on the board. Ask students to provide additional examples to fit the pattern. Then have students open their books to study the chart.

- Have students repeat chorally, or call on individuals to read the questions/sentences in the chart.

- Use the chart to conduct a substitution drill. Call on individuals to say the sentences using, for example, a different verb.

- Use the chart for structured question-and-answer practice; that is, have one student ask a question using the words in the chart and another student give an appropriate answer.

- Have students write additional examples for the chart.

Usage Charts

Some charts, like the one that follows, contain usage notes on the left and example sentences on the right, with the target language in bold. Here are some possibilities for teaching usage charts.

| a. Use subject pronouns to replace nouns in the subject position. | **Alison** wants to be more fit. **She** is taking an exercise class. |
| b. Use object pronouns to replace nouns in the object position. | Sara loves **exercise classes**. She takes **them** three times a week. |

- Discuss each usage note and read the example sentences. Ask students to identify texts or conversations where they encounter the target language. For example, the imperative is often found in recipes and instructions. Elicit the target grammar by asking students questions. To check imperative forms, for example, you may ask, *Can anyone tell me how to make coffee?*
- Write a variety of examples on the board for each usage note (or distribute the examples on paper to students). Ask students to work in pairs to match the usage notes from the chart with the new examples.
- Ask students to work in small groups to come up with an additional example for each note. You can add challenge by asking students to incorporate the unit theme and any target vocabulary.

Additional Presentation Strategies

Photos and Art

Use pictures from magazines or the Internet. Talk about a picture using the target language. (*I think that before they got in the car, they had dinner at a nice restaurant. Now they're going to drive to the beach. They **have driven** down this road many times.*) Use a different picture to elicit the target language from students. (*What happened before this picture? What's going to happen next? What have they already done?*)

Time lines

Use time lines to talk about tenses. List events on the time line and ask questions to elicit the target grammar (*What can you tell me about this person? How long has Maria had her job?*).

Unit-by-Unit Teaching Suggestions

Refer to the Teaching Suggestions for each unit for help with potential trouble spots with the specific target grammar, exceptions to the rules, and unit-specific chart presentation activities.

Grammar Application

This section follows each *Grammar Presentation* and gives students practice with the target grammar in a variety of contexts. The exercises progress from more controlled to more open-ended practice and incorporate the use of all four major skills (reading, writing, listening, speaking). Opportunities for personalization are also offered. A *Data from the Real World* box may be included as well, providing students with an opportunity to practice common real-life uses of the grammar point, giving them tools to make their English sound more natural.

This section of the Student's Book practices the target grammar in a variety of theme-related contexts. The recurring exercise types are listed below with classroom strategies given for each. See the Unit-by-Unit Teaching Suggestions for specific writing, speaking, and other expansion activities as well as suggestions for incorporating the use of technology.

Multiple Choice, Sentence Completion, and Matching Activities

For these activities, have students work individually. To ensure that students are processing the information and to expand on the activities, ask them to do one or more of the following:

- Explain the choice they made using information from the usage chart.
- Check and discuss their answers with a partner.
- Put another example on the board for their classmates to complete.

Listening Activities

Follow these steps with the listening activities.

1. Direct students to read the activity before they listen to help prepare them for what they will hear. To make the activity more challenging, have them guess the answers before listening.
2. Play the audio once all the way through at normal speed. Be sure to tell students that you will play it again. Then play it again, pausing after each item if students need time to finish writing. Play it a third time, again at normal speed.
3. When you reach the end of the exercise, direct students to read through it again. You may want students to compare their answers with a partner's so that they can check for potential errors.
4. Go over the answers by having students write them on the board (one student can write four or five answers), or project the exercise with an overhead or LCD projector, and complete it together.

Scramble Activities

Have students write the answers on the board. Tell them to be sure they haven't left out any words. They can do this by counting the number of words in the scramble activity and making sure it matches the number of words in their completed sentence.

Writing Activities

In these activities, students write or complete sentences with their own ideas. Be sure that they receive feedback on their work. Try one or more of these techniques:

- Have students share their sentences in small groups and then complete the activity on poster paper or on a regular piece of paper, choosing at least one sentence from each member. Post each group's paper so that other students can move around and see it. Tell students to find errors and correct them. Choose global errors to put on the board and discuss in depth with the entire class.
- Have students put sentences on the board. While they are writing, walk around and spot-check the work of other students.

Data from the Real World

These boxes contain research-based usage information, informed by the world's largest corpus. Go over them with the students. Where appropriate, ask for additional examples and discuss students' own impressions or "real world" experiences with the target language.

For example, if the box says, "You can use *someone* with imperatives: *Someone turn off the lights,*" ask students where they might hear this sentence (*in a classroom, at work*). Ask students for additional examples.

The Unit-by-Unit Teaching Suggestions provide additional activities for practice of the information in these boxes.

Avoid Common Mistakes

This section presents a few of the most common learner errors associated with the target grammar, based on the world's largest error-coded learner corpus. It develops students' awareness of common mistakes and gives them an opportunity to practice identifying and correcting these errors in an editing exercise.

The information in this section is based on an extensive database of authentic student writing, so you can be sure that the errors indicated are truly high-frequency. This later gives students an editing focus. If you see these mistakes during unit activities (or even after you've moved on to later units), rather than correcting them yourself, refer students to the box in this section. The Unit-by-Unit Teaching Suggestions often provide further examples of common mistakes.

Editing Task

Have students work individually to complete the task and then compare answers with a partner. Do one of the following to correct the task.

- Once the task is complete, ask two or more students to read the corrected version aloud. Be sure to call on different students each time, so everyone feels accountable.
- Use an LCD or overhead projector to have students work together to correct it.
- Let students know if they miss a mistake, and tell them the category it falls under in the *Avoid Common Mistakes* box. Ask them to search the paragraph again.

Grammar for Writing

This section provides an assignment designed to support students as they learn to incorporate the target grammar in their own writing.

The Grammar for Writing box contains a quick review of the unit grammar as it relates to the writing assignment. Use the following strategies to teach each stage of this section.

Pre-writing Task

Follow these steps to complete the exercise:

1. Go over the information in the box, and tell students they will be focusing on these points for both the practice activity and the writing task.
2. Have students complete the practice activity individually and ask them to compare their answers with a partner.
3. Ask student for the answers. If possible, type the answers using a computer connected to an LCD projector, or write the answers on a copy of the page projected with an overhead projector.

Writing Task

Refer to the Unit-by-Unit Teaching Suggestions for unit-specific ideas and/or alternative writing tasks. Follow these steps for the activities in the book:

1. Help students come up with ideas in one of the following ways.
    - Ask questions to facilitate a whole-class brainstorming session. (*What does the writer of the* Practice *paragraph say about this topic? What are some things you might say about it?*)
    - Seat students in groups, and have each group brainstorm. Then have the groups share their ideas with the class.
2. Draw students' attention to features of the *Practice* paragraph, such as indentations, word choice, or use of the target grammar. Ask them to use the same features in their writing.
3. Assign the writing task as homework, or give students time to finish it in class. If you are doing the activity in class, set a time limit to help students stay on task.

Self- and Peer Editing

The following are strategies for encouraging both self- and peer editing.

- Have students read the editing tips in 2. *Self-Edit* and ask them to read through their writing and make changes as necessary.
- Have students exchange papers with a partner. Ask the partners to underline examples of the target language and check it against the *Avoid Common Mistakes* box. Have them circle any errors. Tell the partners to discuss any mistakes they found before they return the papers for revision.
- Have students peer-edit in groups of three, focusing on one paper at a time.
- Collect the students' writing and note the errors the students circle (or circle any mistakes with the target language that you see). Use these as examples in a follow-up lesson by writing the circled sentences on the board or typing them up and projecting them for class correction.

Grouping Strategies

It is difficult to overestimate the value of using a variety of grouping strategies in the classroom. In addition to making the class more dynamic, it helps you address different learning styles. Time for individual work is important because it allows students to process material in their own ways, but there are also many advantages to pair and group work.

Setting Up Groups

- **To create random groups,** pass out "four of a kind" items, such as colored slips of paper or playing cards. Then ask students to stand, and guide them to different areas of the room: *Everyone with a blue paper, come over here.* Alternatively, you can have students count off by threes or fours. Once they've counted, ask for a show of hands. (*All Number 1s, raise your hands.*) Then have all students with the same number sit together. *Advantage:* Helps build classroom community, challenges students to "get out of their shells," and increases the energy level of the class.
- **To create mixed-level groups,** use items that represent two or more levels. For example, pass out blue cards to higher-level students (or students who performed best on an assessment) and white cards to lower-level students. Tell students to form groups consisting of, for example, two blue cards and two white cards. *Advantage:* Allows for peer tutoring, gives lower-level students exposure to higher-level English, helps lower-level students feel like an integral part of the class.
- **To create same-level groups,** use the same strategy as for mixed-level groups (items to represent levels). Tell students to form groups of all white cards or all blue cards. *Advantage:* Allows you to tailor the activity to the level of the group (by simplifying it for the lower-level group or by making it more challenging/open-ended for the higher-level group).

Pair Work

- For pair work that involves collaborative work, you may want to pair students of similar levels so that one isn't doing all of the work. Or pair students of different levels and give each partner a distinct role. (*Partner A says the question, and Partner B writes it down.*)
- For pair-work activities that encourage repetition, like interviews and surveys, conduct a "walk-around." Have students walk around the room and ask questions to multiple classmates.

Strategies for Multi-level Classrooms

Every class has students at different levels, whether the class is designated "multi-level" or not. Following are some ways to help lower- and higher-level students within multi-level contexts. It is important to use a variety of strategies to address different student needs. Too much separation of lower-level students may make them feel as though they don't belong in the class, and too much peer tutoring may be frustrating for higher-level students.

Lower-level Students

Use one or more of these techniques for working with lower-level students:

- Adapt activities for lower-level students so that they can focus on one task. For example, provide a word bank so they only need to choose the word that belongs in a particular blank, or provide a sentence frame so they only need to supply, for example, the verb.
- Seat students in mixed-level groups and assign an easier role for lower-level students (for example, the reporter who reads the group's answers to the class).

Higher-level Students

- Provide more open-ended tasks for these students after they have completed the exercises in the book (for example, write sentences based on the grammar chart).
- Group higher-level students and give them a special project to complete while you work with lower-level students (for example, write a story using four words from the Academic Word List and at least two examples of the grammar point).

Class Audio Script

Unit 1

Exercise 2.2: Frequency Adverbs
(p. 7 / track 2)

Alex	Hi, Karen. Do you want to go to the mall after class?
Karen	Oh, I hardly ever shop at the mall now.
Alex	Do you shop online?
Karen	Yes. I always shop online. I don't like to stand in line, so shopping online is perfect for me.
Alex	Oh. I never shop online. My Internet connection is really slow. So, what do you buy online?
Karen	Sometimes I buy clothes.
Alex	What else?
Karen	Um, I often buy shoes.
Alex	What else do you do online?
Karen	Lots of things. I read the newspaper, and I usually pay my bills online.
Alex	You do?
Karen	Yeah. I never use stamps. I just move my money from the bank and pay the bill. You should try it!
Alex	That sounds like a really good idea. I always go to the post office. I hate it!

Unit 2

Exercise 3.3: More Simple Present or Present Progressive?
A (p. 24 / track 3)

Large corporations often need to make decisions about new products. Do people want this product? At the present moment, are people looking for a product like this in the stores? New products cost a lot of money and need a lot of research. Corporations usually pay experts to do market research. But there is another way. One large corporation is trying a new idea this year. Every time the company needs market information for a new product, managers ask the employees for their opinions. The employees vote yes or no on the new idea. They tell the managers, "I like the idea" or "I don't like the idea."

Manager Rick Jons said, "Right now we are using the collective brain of our employees, and it seems to work. The results are more reliable than expensive market research."

Unit 3

Exercise 3.1: Imperatives with *Let's* and *Let's Not*
B (p. 36 / track 4)

A	OK, group, Let's think of two more questions.
B	Wait a minute. How will we distribute the questionnaire to everyone?
A	Let's not worry about that now. We can ask the teacher for help when we're ready.
B	I have some ideas for the presentation. Let's talk about that.
A	Let's just finish the questionnaire first. We still need two more questions.
C	Let's see. How about: How many text messages do you send in a day?
A	Great question. One more.
B	What about: Do you sleep with your cell phone near you?
A	I love it! That's six questions. Let's stop there for today, OK? Can we meet again on Thursday or Friday?
C	Let's not meet on Friday. I have to work all day. Thursday's good. Same time?
A	OK, let's meet on Thursday.

Unit 4

Exercise 2.2: Pronunciation Focus: Simple Past *-ed* Endings
(p. 46 / track 5)

Verbs ending in /t/ or /d/ If the base form of the verb ends with the sound /t/ or /d/, say -*ed* as an extra syllable /ɪd/ or /əd/.	**/ɪd/ or /əd/** /t/ rent – rented /d/ decide – decided
Verbs ending in voiceless consonants If the base form of the verb ends in /f/, /k/, /p/, /s/, /ʃ/, and /tʃ/, say the -*ed* as /t/.	**/t/** /f/ lau**gh** – laughed /k/ loo**k** – looked /p/ sto**p** – stopped /s/ mi**ss** – missed /ʃ/ fini**sh** – finished /tʃ/ wat**ch** – watched
Verbs ending in voiced consonants or vowels If the base form of the verb ends in a voiced consonant or vowel, say the -*ed* endings as /d/.	**/d/** li**ve** – lived cha**nge** – changed lea**rn** – learned pl**ay** – played

A (p. 46 / track 6)

rent; rented
decide; decided
laugh; laughed

look; looked
stop; stopped
miss; missed
finish; finished
watch; watched
live; lived
change; changed
learn; learned
play; played

B (p. 46 / track 7)

1. My family moved here six years ago.
2. I needed to earn some money, so I decided to get a job in a factory.
3. I earned a lot of money, but I wanted to be my own boss.
4. I studied business and learned how to start a company.
5. I finished the program and graduated two years ago.
6. Finally, I started my own business.

Exercise 3.1: Statements
B (p. 50 / track 8)

Sarah Breedlove McWilliams Walker was the first American female self-made millionaire. However, before she became a millionaire, life wasn't easy for young Sarah. Her parents died, and Sarah was an orphan at the age of 7. For a time, Sarah and her sister were cotton pickers. By the age of 14, Sarah was already married. Her husband died two years later, and she went to live with her brothers. They were barbers in St. Louis.

In the 1890s, Sarah lost some of her hair. At that time, there were no good products in the stores for this problem. In fact, there weren't a lot of hair care products for African Americans in those days. Sarah worked for a hair product company for a while in Denver. Sarah saw that there was an opportunity for a new business, so she invented "Madam Walker's Wonderful Hair Grower." The business grew. Soon there were other "Madam Walker" products such as shampoos and cosmetics, and she employed over 3,000 people. She started a school to train people to sell her products. She was very successful and eventually became a millionaire.

Unit 5

Exercise 2.3: Answering Questions with Time Clauses
A and B (pp. 57 and 58 / track 9)

Interviewer	Today, I'm talking to Mike Ruiz. Mike is the inventor of a new printer. This printer is very small and light, so you can take it with you when you travel. His new printer has made life easier for millions of business travelers.
	OK, let's start at the beginning. . . . Mike, you were born in Juarez, Mexico, correct?
Mike	Yes.
Interviewer	When did you come to the United States?

Mike	After I graduated from high school.
Interviewer	You went to college here in the States, correct?
Mike	Yes.
Interviewer	So, when did you get the idea for your invention?
Mike	Uhm, when I was a student in college.
Interviewer	And how long did you study at college?
Mike	Until I got my degree.
Interviewer	When did you build your first printer?
Mike	After I graduated from college. I built it with my partner, Ana Ramirez.
Interviewer	And when did you start your printer company?
Mike	As soon as we got the money to start – the funding, you know.
Interviewer	So, when did you get the money for your company?
Mike	Oh, after I presented my idea to some banks and investors. I was really nervous about that, but they all liked it.
Interviewer	And when did the company start making a profit?
Mike	As soon as my first printer reached the stores. It was an immediate success.

Unit 6

Exercise 2.3: More Statements and Questions
A (p. 73 / track 10)

1. The most important day in my life was April 25, 2005. On that day, I was starting school in the United States. I was studying English for the first time. I was feeling nervous. But also, I was feeling hopeful.
2. The most important day in my life was June 3, 2009. On June 3, I was finally getting my driver's license. I was feeling very excited.
3. The most important time in my life was in the spring of 1999. I was leaving home and coming to the United States. I was thinking about my family and missing them.

Unit 7

Exercise 3.2: Measurement Words
B (p. 90 / track 11)

A lot of supermarket shoppers have store club cards these days. Club cards give you lower prices or points for shopping. To get the lower prices, you swipe your card every time you make a purchase. The card tells the store who you are and what you buy. Here is an example. Shopper 1 buys three loaves of bread, two cartons of juice, a gallon of milk, a tube of toothpaste, a package of rice, a bar of soap, and two boxes of cereal each week. What does that tell the store? It probably tells the store that he has a big family, and he probably has children. Shopper 2 buys seven bottles of water, seven cans of tuna, and a pound of turkey each week. What does this tell the store? Shopper 2 is probably single, and she is probably dieting or is concerned with her health. How does the store use this information? It sends advertising to the shoppers with specific information about the products that they buy. This gets them back into the store to buy more products.

Unit 8

Exercise 2.3: *A / An, The,* or No Article?
B (p. 97 / track 12)

Public relations (PR) firms create publicity for companies. For example, a PR person writes an interesting story about a company and tries to get the story into a newspaper. PR firms also try to get people on TV or on the radio to talk about the company. PR firms like to use these media. However, today, they also get their stories into new media, for example, on social networking sites or in blogs. PR firms often hire young people to help them do this. For example, while Ali Lewis, a 25-year-old from Boston, was in college, he wrote a popular blog about the media. A public relations firm read his blog and asked him to come in for a job interview. Ali is a good writer, and he understands how new media work, so they gave him the job. In his new job, Ali helps companies work with social networking sites and blogs.

Unit 9

Exercise 3.2: *To* and *For* with Direct Objects
B (p. 112 / track 13)

Is it possible to change the way you think? Sometimes. Take Ken, for example. Ken was a biology student at a community college. Ken had very strong opinions about a lot of things. He argued with the other students a lot. One day, Ken's teacher, Mrs. Green, gave an exam to the class. The exam tested the students' ability to support their opinions with facts. When Mrs. Green showed the test results to Ken, he was shocked. The results showed that he didn't always base his ideas on correct information. Ken then decided to challenge himself, and Mrs. Green helped Ken. First, she found a website for Ken. It published articles on ideas that were different from Ken's. It was a free website, and the articles were very interesting. Ken discussed the articles with Mrs. Green. Mrs. Green also made quizzes for Ken on the articles he read. Ken did very well on the quizzes. In addition, Mrs. Green found a critical thinking skills class for Ken. He attended the class regularly and kept notes for Mrs. Green. He also e-mailed some reports on the class to Mrs. Green. Today, Ken has excellent critical thinking skills. Both he and Mrs. Green are very proud.

Unit 10

Exercise 2.2: Questions and Answers
A and B (pp. 120 and 121 / track 14)

Chris Green	My guest today is Dr. Marty Robles. Dr. Robles is the president of Rain Forest Biotech. Rain Forest Biotech has made some exciting discoveries in the rain forests of the Amazon. Dr. Robles, you have an exciting company, and you've had an exciting life, too, I think. Tell us a little bit about your life. How many times have you been to the Amazon?
Dr. Robles	I've made 100 trips to the Amazon region.
Chris Green	Who has gone with you?
Dr. Robles	My team.
Chris Green	And who else have you worked with there?
Dr. Robles	Well, I've met many traditional healers on my trips. These people have taught me how they use local plants to cure diseases. I've learned a great deal about their lives and about their land, too.
Chris Green	Have you been to Africa?
Dr. Robles	No, I haven't been to Africa, but my team has visited New Guinea, and I've done research in Australia.
Chris Green	Where else have you been?
Dr. Robles	I've traveled to rain forests in Central America.
Chris Green	What kinds of medicines have you found?
Dr. Robles	My team has discovered medicines for heart disease and diabetes.
Chris Green	You have a busy professional life. How do you find time to be with your family?
Dr. Robles	I've brought my kids with me on some of my expeditions. We've traveled to Costa Rica together, and a few other places.

Unit 11

Exercise 2.2: More Adverbs
B (p. 132 / track 15)

Have you ever noticed that groups of cows all face the same way? Scientists have never been able to explain this. Satellite photos have recently shown that cows around the world all face either north or south. Scientists have still not learned why cows do this. One theory involves magnets. The Earth is like a huge magnet, and magnets point to the north. Studies have already shown that this helps some small animals, such as bats, find their way. In addition, researchers have already found that fish and whales have tiny magnetic particles in their brains. Therefore, some researchers have recently guessed that cows also have magnetic particles in their brains. However, they have not found any proof yet. They still have not done any tests to see if cows have magnetic particles in their brains.

Unit 12

Exercise 3.2: Present Perfect, Present Perfect Progressive, or Both?
B (p. 148 / track 16)

There have been a lot of changes in my neighborhood in the last year. Some changes have been good. For example, four new restaurants have opened. The city has been building a new children's playground, and it should be ready next month. They have also built some green apartments – they finished them six months ago. A lot of new people have moved in already.

Unfortunately, some things have been getting worse. About six stores have closed down, just on my street. Two of my favorite stores have gone out of business. Also, crime has been increasing. Thieves have broken into the deli on my street twice in the last six months. I guess both good and bad things can happen at the same time.

Unit 13

Exercise 2.2: Using Adjectives
A and B (pp. 155 and 156 / track 17)

Nick	I hear you have a new job.
Annie	Yes. I'm a technician at PC Emporium.
Nick	That's great. What are your hours?
Annie	We work 40 hours a week.
Nick	And do you get a vacation?
Annie	Yes. Even new employees get a long vacation – two weeks.
Nick	That sounds fantastic! Do they train you?
Annie	Sure. I'm taking an interesting training course right now. It goes for three days.
Nick	Everything sounds great!
Annie	Not everything. We have to wear an ugly uniform. I wear cotton pants and a sport shirt. The pants are black and the shirt is beige. Oh, and black shoes.
Nick	Running shoes?
Annie	No! Leather shoes.

Unit 14

Exercise 3.4: Listening for Adverbs of Degree
A (pp. 172 and 173 / track 18)

Alison	So, what are some tips for studying and getting good grades?
Dinh	Well, it's important to study really hard.
Alison	Right. It's also pretty important to do all of your homework. What do you think, Carlos?
Carlos	Um, my vocabulary notebook is so helpful to me!
Alison	How does that help?
Carlos	When I want to use a new word, my notebook has sentences to help me remember how to use it.
Dinh	Hmm, I don't know ...
Carlos	Oh, it works amazingly well, in my opinion!

Dinh	OK. So, a vocabulary notebook is a really good idea.
Alison	Yes. So we have three tips. Study, do your homework, and keep a vocabulary notebook. What else?
Dinh	Asking questions! Ask questions in class! That's kind of important.
Carlos	Here's another one: I think it's a really good idea to have a study group. It's incredibly important to have people to study with and to talk about class with, in my opinion.
Dinh	I agree! Studying together is so helpful!

Unit 15

Exercise 3.2: Pronunciation Focus
(p. 183 / track 19)

Some common prepositions have two pronunciations: a strong form and a weak form.		Strong Form	Weak Form
	at	/æt/	/ət/
	for	/fɔːr/	/fər/
	from	/frʌm/ or /frɑm/	/frəm/
	of	/ʌv/ or /ɑv/	/əv/
	to	/tuː/	/tə/
Use the weak form in informal conversation, when you speak quickly and naturally.		*Let's go **to** the supermarket.* *These tomatoes are **from** Florida.*	
Use the strong form: • when you speak formally, slowly, and carefully • when you need to stress the preposition • when the preposition is at the end of the sentence • with *to* when the next sound is a vowel sound		*Welcome **to** this presentation of my work.* *I was driving to the store, not **from** the store.* *Where do these peaches come **from**?* *Let's go **to** a farmers' market.*	

A (p. 184 / track 20)

1.
A Are they from [frəm] California?
B No.
2.
A So, where're they from [frʌm]?
B From [frəm] Georgia.
3.
A Is that a box of [əv] apples?
B No, it's a box of [əv] tomatoes.
4.
A I'll see you at [ət] the restaurant.
B No, let's go to [tə] the cafeteria.
5.
A Who is this peach for [fɔːr]?
B It's for [fər] you. Enjoy!

6.

A   Are you going to [tə] the supermarket today?

B   No, we're going to [tu:] a farmers' market.

Exercise 3.3: Prepositions of Place, Manner, and Logical Relationships

A and B (pp. 184 and 185 / track 21)

Good morning. My talk today is about merchandising. Supermarkets position items carefully. They place things in refrigerator cases, on shelves, and even at the checkout stand. This is called *merchandising*.

Merchandising helps supermarkets sell more items to people in the store. For example, they put candy with other food items, so children ask for the candy when their parents are buying other things. Supermarkets also place certain items near the floor. They put them in a place that children can see easily. For example, they put items children want on the lower shelves. And have you ever noticed kitchen gadgets between the food items on the shelves? This is another example of merchandising.

Supermarkets also place items like magazines at the checkout stands. People see them when they are waiting in line and put them into their carts. In addition, research shows that people buy more cold items, for example, juice or cheese, when the refrigerated shelves are open. That's because they can see what is on them.

So, next time you're waiting in line at the checkout stand, ask yourself, "Why did I buy this? Was it because I needed it, or just because I saw it?" Even as careful shoppers, we all sometimes put things we don't need in our carts.

Unit 16

Exercise 2.3: *Be Going To,* Present Progressive, or Simple Present?

A and B (p. 197 / track 22)

Anne   So, Jin, what are you going to do this weekend?

Jin   I'm finally accomplishing one of my big goals: I'm riding in a hot-air balloon.

Anne   Wow! Did you already make a reservation?

Jin   Yes. I'm taking the flight that goes over the ocean.

Anne   The ocean! You're going to have a great time.

Jin   Yeah, and I heard the weather report. It's going to be great this weekend. Do you want to come?

Anne   When are you going?

Jin   We're meeting in the park at noon on Sunday, and the flight leaves at 1:00 p.m.

Anne   I'd love to come, but I have other plans.

Jin   What are you doing?

Anne   I'm going to the airport on Sunday afternoon. I'm picking up an old friend. She's staying with me for a week, and her flight arrives right at noon.

Jin   Well, it sounds like you're going to have a good time, too!

Unit 17

Exercise 2.3: *Will*: Questions, Answers, and Adverbs

A and B (p. 207 / track 23)

Man   So, Sara, how long do you think you'll live?

Sara   I'll probably live to be about 85 or 90.

Man   Why do you think that?

Sara   Because my grandmother lived to be 85.

Man   Will you work in your 80s?

Sara   I'll undoubtedly work in my 80s.

Man   What kind of job will you have at that age?

Sara   I'll probably have the same job I have now.

Man   Hmm. So what will you do after retirement?

Sara   I'll possibly travel or garden.

Man   But will you have enough money to travel?

Sara   That's a good point. I very likely won't have enough money!

Man   Will you get Social Security?

Sara   No, I certainly won't get Social Security.

Man   Why won't you get Social Security?

Sara   The government undoubtedly won't have any money left in the future!

Man   You're probably right.

Unit 18

Exercise 3.1: Future Conditionals

(pp. 221 and 222 / track 24)

Bob Diaz   Edna is a mature female ape. Researchers are going to try to find out if they can teach Edna to communicate. We asked Dr. Sheila Viss, one of the researchers, about the study. Dr. Viss, if you teach Edna, will she learn human language?

Dr. Viss   That is what we hope to find out. First, if we use American Sign Language, Edna will learn the meaning of some signs. For example, we think Edna will use the sign for "more" if she wants more food.

Bob Diaz   If Edna learns a sign that works in one situation, will she use the same sign in a different situation?

Dr. Viss   Yes. For example, we think Edna will make the sign for a toy when she wants a different toy.

Bob Diaz   So, if she wants something special, will she combine the signs?

Dr. Viss   We think she will. If she does this, Edna will make simple sentences. For example, when she wants food quickly, she will make the signs for "give-food-hurry."

Bob Diaz   When she learns to communicate, will she learn quickly?

Dr. Viss   Well, probably not. Edna will learn slowly compared to a human child.

Exercise 3.3: Time Clauses and Future Conditionals

A (p. 224 / track 25)

Woman	Why are you here at the community college, Jawad?
Jawad	Well, if I speak, read, and write English well, I'll be successful. And if I get a certificate, I'll get a good job.
Woman	True. What are your plans?
Jawad	If I do well in my English classes, I'll apply for a certificate program at the community college. When I finish the certificate program, I'll apply for a good job.
Woman	How will you feel when you finish the program?
Jawad	When I graduate and get my certificate, I'll feel very proud.

Unit 19

Exercise 2.2: *Can* and *Can't*: Questions and Answers

B and C (p. 232 / track 26)

Woman 1	Good morning. I'm here to demonstrate some of the inventions we are going to see in our hospitals in the near future. Today I want to show you the nurse robots we are developing. Before we look at them, though – are there any questions?
Woman 2	Yes – what can these robots do? I mean, can they do everything that a human nurse can do?
Woman 1	They can do a lot of things. And I'm going to talk about that in a moment. To answer your second question, though – they can't do everything that a human nurse can. For example they can't change beds.
Woman 2	Can they speak?
Woman 1	Yes, they can. They can speak quite well.
Woman 2	How many languages can they understand?
Woman 1	So far, they can understand eight languages.
Man	And – can they lift patients?
Woman 1	Yes, they can. For example, they can move patients from beds to wheelchairs.
Man	So, how much weight can one robot lift?
Woman 1	They can lift up to 134 pounds. They can't lift very heavy patients right now.
Man	Can a robot recognize people?
Woman 1	Yes. It can recognize patients, doctors, and other nurses.
Man	Can they give medicine to people?
Woman 1	Yes, they can, but they can't change a patient's medicines.
Man	What kinds of decisions can they make?
Woman 1	So far they can make very simple decisions. For example they can call a doctor in an emergency. Now, let's go look at the nurse robot prototypes we've got....

Unit 20

Exercise 2.2: Formal Requests for Permission

A and B (p. 244 / track 27)

Simon	Professor Brown? Could I ask you a question, please?
Prof. Brown	Hi Simon. Sure. What can I do for you?
Simon	Well, we're having a Halloween party on Wednesday evening.
Prof. Brown	Nice.
Simon	So I was wondering, could I leave class early on Wednesday?
Prof. Brown	How early?
Simon	Only about 15 minutes. I want to pick up the food.
Prof. Brown	Well . . . we have a lot to do on Wednesday, but all right. I guess you can ask a classmate about the last 15 minutes.
Simon	Thank you. The other thing is, do you mind if we use the computer room?
Prof. Brown	What? For the party?
Simon	No. We need a place to change into our costumes and the computer room is ideal because it has no windows.
Prof. Brown	Oh, I see. Yes, that's fine.
Simon	And do you mind if we borrow your CD player? I mean for the music.
Prof. Brown	No, not at all. That's fine. Sounds like it'll be a great party.
Simon	We hope so, and so I wanted to ask: do you mind if we give you our homework on Friday, not Thursday?
Prof. Brown	No, no problem. And so can I ask a question?
Simon	Sure.
Prof. Brown	Could I come to your party?
Simon	Oh, yes, of course! We'd love you to come.

Exercise 3.2: Formal and Informal Offers and Responses

A (p. 248 / track 28)

1.

A	Hi, Tony. I'll drive to the raffle tonight. OK?
B	Oh, that would be great. Thanks.

2.

A	Sarah, we can help you carry those bags.
B	OK, thanks. They're really heavy.

3.

A	Could I help you move those tables, Mr. Lee?
B	No, thank you. I just finished.

4.

A	Can I put the snacks and drinks out now?
B	Yes, please. Thanks!

5.

A	Jordy, we'll help you take tickets.
B	OK, thanks.

6.

A Ms. Moncur, may I help you with the decorations?

B Yes, please. Thank you.

7.

A Oh, no!

B I can clean it up.

A Thanks!

8.

A Can I finish that for you, Paula?

B Yes, thank you.

Unit 21

Exercise 2.2: Asking for and Giving Advice
C (p. 259 / track 29)

1. Arthur had better not take the job and move. It sounds like he might be unhappy if he does. This is a difficult decision, but he needs to consider what is more important to him – friends and family or the perfect job.
2. Ari should probably talk to a career counselor. A counselor could help him figure out what he wants.
3. Maybe Camilla ought to take the job. If she really needs money, she could take the job and continue looking for another one.
4. Perhaps Samuel should look for another job, but still keep this job. He really shouldn't quit this job before he has another one.
5. Yes, Eleni really ought to do some volunteer work. It's a great way to find out if you really are interested in another field.
6. Katya should really start talking to people and getting information. She should get information about any job or field that seems interesting to her.
7. I think Terry had better start looking for another job. It doesn't sound good, but he should probably talk to his boss, too. Maybe there is a problem that he can solve.
8. Helen ought to do what makes her happy. She's an adult now.

Unit 22

Pronunciation Focus: *Have To, Has To, Have Got To*
(p. 269 / track 30)

In informal conversation . . .

have to is often pronounced "hafta."

has to is often pronounced "hasta."

got to is often pronounced "gotta."

Exercise 2.1: Statements
A (p. 269 / track 31)

Good morning, everyone. Thanks for coming. I know we're all excited about our new project to create three new advertisements together. But we've got to do this quickly, so we really have to work together. Here are a few points to get us started:

First of all, you'll work in teams of four. I'll hand out the team assignments in a few minutes. Each team needs to choose a leader. The leader has to organize the team. We have some time scheduled tomorrow for you to do this.

Then, you'll all need to work together to make a plan for the project. I know that might take a few days, but please send me your plan as soon as possible. I absolutely must have all plans by the end of the week.

A point for team leaders: We have four weeks to complete this project. You really must e-mail a report of your progress to me at the end of each week. The report doesn't have to be long, but it needs to explain your progress clearly. You can't forget this because I need to report to the president every week. I'll remind you.

OK – Now, one final point. The most important of all, really. Be creative! We've got to create some really interesting ads. But remember, we must be honest in all of the ads. That's an important rule.

I think that's everything for right now. Do you have any questions? No? OK then! Let me get you those team assignments. . . .

Unit 23

Exercise 2.1: Present Probability
A and B (pp. 281 and 282 / track 32)

Man	I read an interesting article today about a new trend. A lot more young adults are moving back home to live with their parents.
Woman	That shouldn't be hard to understand. The economy must be part of the reason, especially for people just out of college. It can't be easy if you have a lot of debt and college loans. And it must be hard for young people to find a good job these days.
Man	Yes, but there could be other reasons too. I've heard that a lot more people are going back to school. So they may not be able to afford an apartment, even if they have jobs. It might be better financially for them to live at home.
Woman	I wonder how easy it is for the parents. It can't always be easy for them. They think they've finished raising their children, but then their children come back home. I guess parents should expect this to happen sometimes, but that doesn't mean it's easy.
Man	Maybe, but it could be nice too. Some parents might like to have their children around as they get older.
Woman	That's true. I guess it could depend on the family.
Man	Of course. It must.

Exercise 3.1: Future Probability
A and B (p. 285 / track 33)

Interviewer	We're talking to Professor Meredith Li today. We're discussing how she thinks schools may or may not be different in the future.

Welcome. Dr. Li, do you think schools will be different in the future?

Dr. Li Oh, there's no doubt. Schools and education will be quite different. The question is how? There may be small changes, or there could be larger ones. But, things will be different. Technology will be the most important thing.

Interviewer How will technology affect education?

Dr. Li Well, it's already an important part of education. Schools have computers, and many students have their own computers, too. And this trend should continue. More and more students should have computers in the future. More interesting, though, is this question: Will we actually need physical schools in the future?

Interviewer What do you mean?

Dr. Li Well, we can access so much information on the Internet. It might not be necessary to have physical schools in the future. It may be more efficient for all students to study from home with their computers. They could see and hear the teacher over the Internet and not actually need to go to school.

Interviewer I've heard this idea before. But, what about all the social aspects of going to school? Won't children still need those?

Dr. Li It's true that learning social skills is an important part of school. But it's possible to learn these skills outside of school. For example, parents and schools could organize social activities in new places. There should be places to do this even if children don't go to an actual school.

Interviewer Hmm. What about books and libraries? Do you think we're still going to have those?

Dr. Li Interesting question. In some ways, we might not need libraries. We can access so much information online! And we can read books electronically, so you could say that paper books are not necessary anymore. But, I'm not sure. There could always be some people who want to read real books and go to real libraries. I may be wrong, but that's what I think.

Interviewer Well, thank you Professor Li. It's been a very interesting discussion. . . .

Unit 24

Exercise 3.1: Verb + Object + Preposition Combinations
(p. 295 / track 34)

Man How was work today?

Woman Good, but it was really busy. I had a meeting with the new employees early this morning. I explained company policies to them.

Man How did that go?

Woman OK, but a few people didn't understand everything. I spent some time with them after the meeting. I discussed everything with them one more time. I think they understood by the end.

Man That's good. It sounds like it took extra time, though.

Woman It did, so I was behind on my other work today. Then, to make matters worse, I had computer problems.

Man Oh no!

Woman Yeah. I couldn't fix them, so I borrowed a laptop from the technology department. I had to work on a presentation for tomorrow. I asked Robert for some information, but he didn't have it. I had to wait and get it from Carrie. That took even more time. I was finally getting started on the presentation when Carrie reminded me about a department meeting at 11:30. So I had to run to that.

Man You were busy!

Woman Yeah. I finally finished the presentation after lunch. Robert and Carrie both had time to help me with it then. We got it done late this afternoon, just in time! I need it early tomorrow morning. I thanked Carrie and Robert for their help, cleaned up my desk a little, and rushed home. What a day! It's nice to relax!

Unit 25

Exercise 3.2: Transitive Phrasal Verbs
(p. 310 / track 35)

Interviewer Dana Wikman is a money expert. Welcome, Dana. Can you give us some simple, basic money strategies?

Dana Yes, definitely. One of the most basic things you can do is just to put away a little money each month. It doesn't even matter how much it is, the point is to get into the habit of saving.

Interviewer OK, so save a little money each month.

Dana Yes, you'll be surprised. Even a small amount will add up over time.

Interviewer What else?

Dana Well, obviously, you need to work out a budget. You won't get anywhere if you don't do that. Write down your expenses. And, don't throw away receipts.

Interviewer OK, you're saying to keep good records.

Dana Exactly. Then you know how much you have and how much you're spending.

Interviewer How about credit card debt?

Dana First, don't build up a lot of debt. If at all possible, pay off your credit card every month. That's the best approach if you can do it.

Interviewer	Now, what about couples? I know money can be a problem for couples sometimes.
Dana	Well, the most important thing is to talk about it. You need to bring the topic up and discuss it. It can be easy to ignore, but that will just create problems. It's important for couples to understand how each person thinks about money.
Interviewer	OK, good advice. I have to say that this all sounds like fairly simple advice.
Dana	Well, it is. The thing is that money management isn't that complex. The problem is doing it. Of course it's hard for people to just do it. So, my last piece of advice is: Don't put off money matters. They are very important.

Unit 26

Exercise 2.1: Comparative Forms
(pp. 317 and 318 / track 36)

A Norwegian study says that there may be differences in intelligence between brothers. The study showed that older siblings are more intelligent than their younger siblings. The researchers gave intelligence tests to 60,000 pairs of brothers. They found that the older siblings did better than their brothers on the tests. The younger boys' scores were definitely worse, although not by very much.

Researchers say one reason for this may be that older siblings have better language skills. Their language may develop more quickly because they have been in an adult environment longer. It is possible that younger siblings are more intelligent in other ways, for example, in emotional intelligence.

The Norwegian study did not look at age differences. However, earlier research suggests that when the age difference between two brothers is bigger, the difference in intelligence is smaller.

Unit 27

Exercise 2.2: More Superlative Forms
A and B (p. 332 / track 37)

Now we're going to talk about a few major disasters in history. We'll consider their impact on society. We'll start by going far back in history.

The first example is the eruption of a volcano in Italy in the year 76 CE. The eruption of Mount Vesuvius is one of the most famous natural disasters in history. It is also probably the most important disaster in history because of what we learned from it about life at that time. The volcanic eruption destroyed two ancient Italian cities. However, the way the ash fell meant that many city structures – for example, homes, markets, and roads – were not destroyed. And we have learned a lot from that. The eruption of Mount Vesuvius was certainly a terrible

disaster. However, it has also been one of the most helpful events in history for archeologists.

The next disaster I want to discuss happened in Chicago in 1871. The Great Chicago Fire lasted three days. It was the biggest fire and the worst disaster in the history of the city. Most of the city was destroyed. There are different stories about how the fire started. The most popular story is that a cow kicked over a lantern in a barn and started the fire. No one knows for sure, though. The way people worked together after the fire was the most interesting result. They rebuilt the city very quickly. They built 300,000 buildings in only three months, and they made the buildings more resistant to fire. I think that has to be one of the fastest building projects in history. This also shows how people often work together the best when they are helping one another. We've also seen this in more recent disasters. We'll discuss those next time. . . .

Unit 28

Exercise 2.1: Listening for Gerunds and Infinitives
(p. 341 / track 38)

Most people feel that time speeds up as they get older. At the end of each day, adults often ask themselves: Why haven't I done the things that I planned to do today?

When you are a child, time seems to go very slowly. As you get older, time tends to pass more quickly. Why do adults and children see time differently?

According to psychologists, one theory is that children tend to look forward. On a car trip, for example, children always want to arrive. They ask, "Are we there yet?" Children look forward, so time seems to last longer. Adults, on the other hand, enjoy looking back and thinking about their memories.

In addition, adults tend to be busy, so time often passes more quickly for them. Also, most adults will keep looking at their watch throughout the day, and as a result, be more aware of time.

Finally, children have a lot of new experiences to process, but as people get older, they do not tend to have so many new experiences. This also speeds time up. Maybe experiencing new adventures as we get older can help us feel as if we can regain a little bit of that childhood sense of time.

Unit 29

Exercise 3.1: Infinitives After *Be,* to Show Purpose, and with *It*
(p. 356 / track 39)

It was very difficult to be a woman in the United States in the early part of the twentieth century. Women did not have many rights. For example, they were not able to vote.

In 1917, Alice Paul organized a group of women to fight for the right to vote in national elections. The group demonstrated in front of the White House in order to get the president's attention. This angered many people. The police arrested many women to stop the demonstrations. However, this didn't work, so they arrested Paul and gave her a 7-month jail sentence in order to frighten the other women. This was unfair, but Alice Paul was strong. She stopped eating. She went on a hunger strike to call attention to the issue of women's rights.

Paul suffered in order to earn the right to vote, but in the end, this and other demonstrations worked. Congress finally gave women the vote in 1920.

Unit 30

Exercise 3.1: Verbs in Subject Relative Clauses
(pp. 368 and 369 / track 40)

Why do we sleep? This is still a mystery. Scientists who study sleep are still not completely sure of the reasons. They know some things about sleep, however. Here are some facts:

- People who are asleep have active brains. Their brains are most active during the "rapid eye movement," or REM, phase of sleep.
- Different animals sleep in different ways. For example, a dolphin that is sleeping may continue to swim.
- Humans and animals that lose sleep need to make it up later on.
- A person who needs less than eight hours of sleep should not worry about sleeping less than other people.
- There are animals that sleep very little. For example, a horse only sleeps three hours a day. There are other animals that sleep a lot. For example, a small animal called a ferret sleeps about 15 hours a day.

Scientists who study sleep also have a few guesses about the reasons for sleep. There is a study that has shown REM sleep helps learning and memory. However, there are other studies that have shown the opposite results. For example, certain drugs shorten REM sleep. A group of people who were taking these drugs showed no memory problems in a recent study.

Most scientists agree on one thing. They need to do more research to solve the mysteries of sleep.

Unit 31

Exercise 3.1: Verbs in Object Relative Clauses
A and B (pp. 380 and 381 / track 41)

A vaccine is a substance that a health practitioner gives to help a person avoid getting a disease. There are two types of flu vaccines. One is a shot that a practitioner usually gives the patient in the arm. The other type is a nasal spray that the practitioner sprays directly into the patient's nose. Scientists develop new flu vaccines every year. They study flu viruses that people around the world had the previous year. Then they choose three critical viruses and make vaccines for them. For example, in 2009, the viruses they chose were the most likely to continue to cause disease in 2010.

People often don't like to get their flu shots. However, the flu shot that scientists developed for 2009 was in high demand in the United States. More people than usual received that shot. According to doctors, getting a flu shot each year is the most important thing a person can do to prevent the flu. Maybe their message is now being heard.

Unit 32

Exercise 2.3: Using *And, Or, But,* and *So*
B (pp. 390 and 391 / track 42)

Interviewer Many people know about Thanksgiving in the United States, but some people might not know about Canadian Thanksgiving. I have with me in the studio Vanessa Speers, who's a native of Toronto. Welcome, Vanessa. So, tell us about Canadian Thanksgiving. What are the differences between the United States and Canada?

Vanessa Well, there are a lot of similarities and some differences. Canadian Thanksgiving is a little older. It started in 1578, but as you know, Thanksgiving started a little later in the United States – in 1621.

In 1578, a man named Martin Frobisher arrived in Canada from Europe and had the first Thanksgiving dinner. In the United States it was English Pilgrims who – or so the history books say – started the tradition. The two Thanksgivings are also on different dates. U.S. Thanksgiving is in November, but in Canada, Thanksgiving is in October. In the United States, Thanksgiving Day is always on a Thursday, but in Canada it's on a Monday. However, both holidays have similar traditions. In both countries people get together with family and have the traditional Thanksgiving dinner; and they both eat turkey and pumpkin pie.

In the United States, the meal is always on a Thursday – that is, on Thanksgiving Day – but in Canada, it can be on one of several days. Canadians can have Thanksgiving dinner on Saturday, Sunday, or Monday. One other difference is that in the United States, Black Friday, the day after Thanksgiving, is the big holiday shopping day, when many things are on sale. Many people have the day off, too. But in Canada, people don't have the day off, so it's not a big shopping day. In Canada, the big sales are a month later, on December 26th, the day after Christmas Day.

Both the U.S. Thanksgiving and the Canadian Thanksgiving are important holidays, but they have minor differences.

Interviewer Thank you, Vanessa. Vanessa Speers there, talking to us about Thanksgiving . . .

Answer Key

1 Simple Present
Are You Often Online?

1 Grammar in the Real World

A page 2

Answers will vary; Possible answer: One bad thing about spending time online is that some people do not spend time together as a family very often. One good thing is that social networking sites help people stay in touch with friends and family who live far away.

B Comprehension Check page 3

Possible answers:

1. Does spending a lot of time with computers and less and less time with people change how people interact with family and friends? Does it help or hurt people and relationships?
2. The average person in the United States spends 13 hours a week online.
3. Face-to-face time is meeting with someone in the same place directly.
4. No. It says to try to balance online time with face-to-face time.

C Notice page 3

1. spend; spend
2. disagree
3. spends
4. helps

Verbs end in -s: sentences 3 and 4.

2 Simple Present
Exercise 2.1 Statements

A page 7

2. use
3. shops
4. check
5. isn't / is not
6. don't / do not buy
7. spends
8. interacts
9. doesn't / does not hurt

B Over to You page 7

Answers will vary.

Exercise 2.2 Frequency Adverbs page 7

2. always
3. never
4. sometimes
5. often
6. usually
7. never
8. always

Exercise 2.3 Time Expressions and Frequency Adverbs page 8

2. every day
3. often
4. on Saturday
5. twice
6. hardly ever
7. always
8. never

Exercise 2.4 Questions

A page 8

2. Do you read the news online?
3. How often do you shop online?
4. Where do you usually check your e-mail?
5. What is your favorite website?
6. Do you sometimes download music?
7. *Answers will vary.*
8. *Answers will vary.*

B Group Work page 9

Answers will vary.

C Pair Work page 9

Answers will vary.

3 Time Clauses and Factual Conditionals
Exercise 3.1 Time Clauses

A pages 10–11

2. After	6. while
3. before	7. while
4. While	8. before
5. As soon as	

B Pair Work page 11

Answers will vary.

Exercise 3.2 Time Clauses and Factual Conditionals page 11

2. (She usually starts with a search engine) when she does research.
3. If the topic is general, (Dani thinks about the best words to put into the search engine.)
4. For example, if the topic is "How to avoid identity theft," (Dani uses *avoid identity theft*.)
5. If she gets too many results, (she puts quotation marks around the words "identity theft.")
6. (She clicks on a result) if it comes from a useful site.
7. When she gets to the page, (she usually skims the information first.)
8. (She reads the entire page) if the information seems useful.

Exercise 3.3 More Factual Conditionals

A page 12

2. f   3. a   4. g   5. d   6. h   7. c   8. b

B Over to You page 12

Answers will vary.

4 Avoid Common Mistakes

Editing Task page 13

My roommate Mark plays online games. He ~~don't~~ *doesn't* own

a computer, so he goes to a computer lab. How often

~~he does~~ *does he* play? He plays every night! As soon as he finishes his

homework‸ *,* he goes to the lab. ~~He does not sometimes~~ *Sometimes he does not / doesn't* come

home until midnight. He usually plays the game with friends

from around the world. He ~~don't~~ *doesn't* know the other players, but it

doesn't matter. When Mark gets home‸ *,* he always has stories

about the games he plays. Why‸ *do* people play these games?

I do not understand. ~~I amn't~~ *I'm not / I am not* like Mark. I always play with

people face-to-face when I play a game. When I play a game‸ *,* I

know the people. ~~Does~~ *Do* many people play online games? How

often ~~you do~~ *do you* play online games?

5 Grammar for Writing
Using Simple Present with Time Clauses

Pre-writing Task

1 page 14

Possible answer: The writer's friends use their cell phones to text people all the time. The writer rarely texts.

2 page 14

My friends can't live without their cell phones. (When they lose their cell phones), they become very nervous and upset. (When I'm with my friends), I feel that they don't always listen to me. I think it's because they text wherever they are. They text at restaurants, at parties, in class, and they even text on dates. Some of my friends send texts (after they go to bed). (As soon as they wake up), they check their messages. I rarely text. I prefer talking with people face-to-face.

Writing Task

1 Write page 15

Answers will vary.

2 Self-Edit page 15

Answers will vary.

2 Present Progressive and Simple Present
Brainpower

1 Grammar in the Real World

A page 16

Answers will vary; Possible answer: They are improving their brains by looking at interesting websites, doing word puzzles, eating blueberries, jogging, and thinking beautiful, calm thoughts.

B Comprehension Check page 17

2. c   3. d   4. a

C Notice page 17

1. is sitting
2. live
3. helps
General: sentences 2 and 3
In progress right now: sentence 1

2 Present Progressive
Exercise 2.1 Statements

A page 19

2. is using
3. is not driving
4. is walking
5. is running
6. are going
7. are trying
8. is not going
9. is not eating

B Over to You page 20

2. My best friend is / is not / 's not / isn't learning a musical instrument.
3. I am / am not / 'm not improving my vocabulary.
4. My friends are / are not / aren't improving their vocabulary.
5. I am / am not / 'm not eating less junk food.
6. My family are / are not / aren't eating less junk food. *OR* My family is / is not / 's not / isn't eat less junk food.
7. I am / am not / 'm not studying math.
8. My co-workers are / are not / aren't studying math.

Exercise 2.2 Questions and Answers

A page 20

1. b. are; doing; *Answers will vary.*
2. a. Are; trying; *Answers will vary.*
   b. are; doing; *Answers will vary.*
3. a. Are; reading; *Answers will vary.*
   b. are; reading; *Answers will vary.*
   c. are; reading; *Answers will vary.*
4. a. Are; getting; *Answers will vary.*
   b. Are; eating; *Answers will vary.*
5. a. Are; taking; *Answers will vary.*
   b. are; studying; *Answers will vary.*
6. a. Are; working; *Answers will vary.*
   b. Are; getting; *Answers will vary.*

B Pair Work page 20

Answers will vary.

C Pair Work page 20

Answers will vary.

3 Simple Present and Present Progressive Compared

Exercise 3.1 Simple Present or Present Progressive? page 22

2. seems
3. has
4. understands
5. loves
6. writes
7. designs
8. owns
9. reads
10. 's / is studying
11. looks
12. likes
13. does not / doesn't spend
14. 's / is playing
15. is having

Exercise 3.2 Stative or Active? page 23

2. have
3. looks
4. think
5. thinking
6. have
7. looking
8. having
9. look

Exercise 3.3 More Simple Present or Present Progressive?

A page 24

3. are; looking
4. cost
5. need
6. pay
7. is trying
8. needs
9. ask
10. vote
11. tell
12. like
13. don't like
14. are using
15. seems

B page 24

2. Are you looking for a better dictionary right now?
3. Are you using a dictionary in this class today?
4. Do you prefer an online dictionary or a paper one?
5. Do you use a dictionary when you prepare for tests?
6. Are you preparing for a test at the moment?

C Group Work page 24

Answers will vary.

4 Avoid Common Mistakes

Editing Task page 25

　　　　　　　　　　　　　　resembles
　　The human brain ~~is resembling~~ a computer. It stores a lot of information. But humans are smarter than computers because we store things outside of our brains that we do not need to store *in* our brains. For example, we
store
~~are storing~~ information in books, newspapers, images, and of course, computers. Another example is this text.
　　　　　　　　　　　reading　　　　　*don't / do not need*
At this moment, you are ~~read~~ this text. You ~~are not needing~~
　　　　　　　　　　　　　　　　　　　　　has
to remember all the information in it. The book ~~is having~~ the information, and you read it when you need it. If
　　　　planning
you are ~~planing~~ an essay, you can make notes on paper
　　　　　　　　　　　　　　　　writing
or on a computer. When you are ~~writting~~ the essay, you
　　　　　　　　　　　　　　studying
can read those notes again. If you are ~~studing~~ a subject, you can go online and find information about it. The information is on the Internet. We do not look into people's
　　　　　　　　　　　　enjoying　　　　　　　*are*
brains to see it. When we are ~~enjoing~~ an online video, we ‸ watching something that is outside of the human brain. So computers are like extensions of our brains.

5 Grammar for Writing

Using Simple Present and Present Progressive Together

Pre-writing Task

1 page 26

These days I **am not taking** [PP] good care of myself. Most of the time I **eat** [SP] healthy foods and I **exercise** [SP], but currently I **am not living** [PP] a healthy lifestyle. I **work** [SP] at a big department store. During the holidays, the store **gets** [SP] very busy. I **do not usually work** [SP] overtime, but this holiday season I **am working** [PP] 16 hours every day. I **am making** [PP] more money, but I **am not getting** [PP] enough sleep because I **am working** [SP] so much. I always **feel** [SP] tired these days. Usually, I **enjoy** [SP] this time of year, but I **do not like** [SP] it this year. I **am looking forward** [PP] to the end of the holiday season.

2 page 26

in progress now	habits
am not living	eat
am working	exercise
am making	work
am not getting	gets
am working	do not usually work
feel	enjoy
am looking forward	do not like

Writing Task

1 Write page 27

Answers will vary.

2 Self-Edit page 27

Answers will vary.

3 Imperatives

What's Appropriate?

1 Grammar in the Real World

A page 28

Answers will vary; Possible answer: Some good rules to follow in an e-mail to a professor include: using an e-mail address that shows your name; writing the purpose of your e-mail in the subject line; starting with a greeting; being brief, clear, and specific; and being polite.

B Comprehension Check page 29

a. A   b. NA   c. NA   d. A   e. A

C Notice page 29

1. **Use** an e-mail address that shows your name.
2. **Always start** with a greeting, for example, "Dear Prof. Smith."
3. **Do not write** pages and pages of text.
4. **Don't use** text messaging abbreviations.

2 Imperatives

Exercise 2.1 Forming Imperatives

A page 31

3. Let
4. don't answer
5. Keep
6. Send
7. Find
8. Don't take; leave

B Over to You page 31

Possible answers:
1. Always turn your cell phone ringer off in the office.
2. Never use a pop song for a ring tone.
3. Always let unimportant calls go to voice mail.
4. If your cell phone rings in a restroom, never answer it!
5. Always keep your voice down.
6. Always send text messages instead of making phone calls.
7. Always find a quiet, private place to take calls, and be brief.
8. Never take a call in a meeting. Always leave the room and take the call outside.

Exercise 2.2 Time Clauses and *If* Clauses page 32

2. When you are in a face-to-face meeting, don't check your messages.
   Don't check your messages when you are in a face-to-face meeting.
3. If you are in a meeting, don't keep checking your messages.
   Don't keep checking your messages if you are in a meeting.
4. When you are in a presentation, don't reply to a call or an e-mail
   Don't reply to a call or an e-mail when you are in a presentation.
5. If you are expecting a call, tell the other people in a meeting.
   Tell the other people in a meeting if you are expecting a call.
6. If you take a phone call in a meeting, leave the room to talk.
   Leave the room to talk if you take a phone call in a meeting.
7. If you leave the room to take a call, be brief.
   Be brief if you leave the room to take a call.

8. After you finish your call and come back to the room, apologize.

Apologize after you finish your call and come back to the room.

Exercise 2.3 Making Rules with Imperatives

A Group Work page 33

Answers will vary.

B Group Work page 33

Answers will vary.

Exercise 2.4 Imperatives with Subject Pronouns

A page 33

2. you do
3. you be; you play
4. don't you worry
5. you be
6. you be; you take
7. you think
8. you find

B page 34

2. Somebody / Someone
3. everybody / everyone
4. Somebody / Someone
5. somebody / someone
6. Somebody / Someone
7. everybody / everyone
8. everybody / everyone

3 Let's . . .

Exercise 3.1 Imperatives with *Let's* and *Let's Not*

A pages 35–36

2. Let's choose a topic
3. let's write down
4. Let's see
5. let's not put it first
6. let's ask

B page 36

2. Let's not worry
3. Let's talk
4. Let's just finish
5. Let's see.
6. Let's stop
7. Let's not meet
8. let's meet

Exercise 3.2 Imperatives with *Let's* and *Let's Not* pages 36–37

3. let's try brainstorming ideas.
4. Let's divide the ideas up so that everyone presents something.
5. Let's not worry about that now.
6. Let's vote on it.
7. Let's stop for now and meet tomorrow.

4 Avoid Common Mistakes

Editing Task page 37

What are the rules for making an appropriate social networking profile? First, ~~dont~~ *don't* use a silly photo of you. Choose a professional-looking photo. For example, ~~no~~ *don't / do not* use a picture of yourself at a party or at the beach. And ~~dont~~ *don't* use a photo that is too old. Update your photo every few years.

For your profile, ~~donot~~ *do not* give too much information. Always remember: Strangers are looking at your profile. Include details that can give possible employers a good impression.

A professional social networking profile is like a résumé, so ~~no~~ *don't / do not* lie in your profile. Always be honest about your experience and your skills.

5 Grammar for Writing

Using Imperatives with Time Clauses, *If*, *Always* and *Never*

Pre-writing Task

1 page 38

Hi Matt,

Your trip to Japan next month sounds wonderful. There are some things you need to know about meeting people and communicating in Japan. <u>Read</u> these instructions. If you have any questions, <u>call</u> me.

1. (Always bring) a gift when you are invited to someone's home. <u>Wrap</u> the gift, and <u>hand</u> it to your hosts with both hands. If your hosts give you a gift, (always accept) it with both hands.

2. If someone invites you to their home, (never wear) shoes inside. <u>Wear</u> socks, and if your hosts give you slippers, <u>put</u> them on. When you put your shoes down, <u>make</u> the toes face the door. (Always take off) the slippers before

you go into the bathroom, though, and <u>put on</u> the special bathroom slippers from your hosts.

3. If you take a train or bus in Japan, (always set) your cell phone to silent mode, or as the Japanese call it, "Manner Mode." (Never talk loudly) on the phone when you are on the train. It will annoy the other passengers. Instead, use e-mail or text messages.

4. If you are near elderly people on public transportation, (always turn off) your cell phone. The electromagnetic waves from the cell phone could affect medical equipment like pacemakers.
<u>Have</u> a fantastic trip! <u>Call</u> me as soon as you get back.
Hikumi

2 page 39

Possible answers:

2. Never accept the gift with one hand.
3. Always wear socks or slippers inside. *OR* Always take off your shoes outside.
4. Always talk quietly on the phone.

Writing Task

1 Write page 39

Answers will vary.

2 Self-Edit page 39

Answers will vary.

4 Simple Past
Entrepreneurs

1 Grammar in the Real World

A page 40

Answers will vary; Possible answer: Google started when Sergey Brin and Larry Page designed a new Internet search engine.

B Comprehension Check page 41

Possible answers:

1. They met at Stanford University.
2. Sergey's roommate complained about the noise from his computers.
3. Google Maps and Gmail are other products started by Google.
4. About 20,000 people worked for Google after 10 years.

C Notice page 41

Group A	Group B
1. started	5. came
2. moved	6. was, were
3. studied	7. became
4. happened	8. met

Group A forms the past by adding *-ed*, while Group B forms the past by changing the word.

2 Simple Past
Exercise 2.1 Statements and Questions

A page 44

2. met	14. stayed
3. graduated	15. went
4. began	16. thought
5. drove	17. chose
6. worked	18. took
7. tried	19. saw
8. didn't / did not graduate	20. didn't / did not have
9. taught	21. found
10. made	22. opened
11. wanted	23. became
12. graduated	24. had
13. applied	25. gave

B Pair Work page 45

2. Did; meet
   No, they didn't.
3. Did; graduate
   No, he didn't.
4. Did; teach
   Yes, he did.
5. Did; go
   Yes, he did.
6. Did; apply
   No, he didn't.
7. Did; think
   No, they didn't.
8. Did; open
   Yes, they did.

C page 45

Possible answers:
2. did Ben and Jerry meet
3. did Jerry teach
4. did Ben and Jerry take
5. did the course cost
6. did Ben and Jerry open their first store
7. did Ben and Jerry's quickly become popular
8. did Ben and Jerry's give away on their first anniversary
   OR did Ben and Jerry's give everyone as a "thank you"

D Pair Work page 46

2. X		6. X	
3. did		7. X	
4. X		8. did	
5. did			

Exercise 2.2 Pronunciation Focus: Simple Past *-ed* Endings

A page 46

No answers.

B page 46

1. My family moved here six years ago.
2. I needed to earn some money, so I decid(ed) to get a job in a factory.
3. I earned a lot of money, but I want(ed) to be my own boss.
4. I studied business and learned how to start a company.
5. I finished the program and graduat(ed) two years ago.
6. Finally, I start(ed) my own business.

C Over to You page 47

Answers will vary.

Exercise 2.3 Questions and Answers

A page 47

2. didn't / did not have	9. graduated
3. learned	10. moved
4. began	11. hosted
5. went	12. started
6. worked	13. became
7. worked	14. grew
8. became	15. became

B Pair Work pages 47–48

Possible answers:
1. did Oprah Winfrey have; She had a difficult childhood.
2. did she learn to do; She learned to read.
3. did she go to; She went to Tennessee State University.
4. did she do; She worked on a radio show.
5. did she do; She worked at a TV station.
6. did she move; She moved to Baltimore.
7. did she start; She started working on a morning show.
8. did it become; In 1986, it became a national show.

3 Simple Past of *Be* and *There Was There Were*

Exercise 3.1 Statements

A page 50

2. wasn't / was not	7. there were
3. was	8. there weren't / were not
4. were	9. there was
5. was	10. there were
6. were	11. was

B Pair Work page 50

Possible answers:
Her brothers were barbers in St. Louis.
Sarah worked for a hair product company for a while in Denver.
Sarah employed over 3,000 people.
She started a school to train people to sell her products.

Exercise 3.2 Questions with *Be* and Other Verbs

A Pair Work page 51

2. Was it a good job?
3. What were your co-workers like?
4. What did you do there?
5. Why did you leave?
6. What was your best job?
7. Why did you like it?
8. Where was your worst job?

B Pair Work page 51

Answers will vary.

4 Avoid Common Mistakes

Editing Task page 52

My family ~~move~~ *moved* from Mexico City to the United States in 1998. I went to Hamilton High School in Los Angeles. I did not ~~knew~~ *know* anybody, and I did not ~~had~~ *have* any friends here. I ~~in 1999~~ *In 1999 OR in 1999.* met Jun‸ *In 1999* He became my first friend. ‸ We ~~in 2001~~ *In 2001, OR in 2001.* graduated‸ I got a job at a nice restaurant, but I did not ~~enjoyed~~ *enjoy* my job. Jun drove a taco truck, but he did not ~~liked~~ *like* the food. I wanted to be my own boss, and I always liked food and cooking. Jun wanted his own business, too. Jun saw an opportunity. There ~~was~~ *were* hungry office workers downtown at noon, but there ~~weren't~~ *wasn't* a nice place to eat. We bought a food truck and we ~~start~~ *started* Food on the Move in 2003. Today, we have 5 trucks and 15 employees.

5 Grammar for Writing

Using Simple Past

Pre-writing Task

1 page 53

No answers

2 page 53

My boss, Missolle, (came) to the United States from Haiti 12 years ago. When she (came) here, she (was) very sad because her children (were) still in Haiti. She (wanted) them to <u>come</u> here, so she (worked) very hard. She (practiced) her English all the time. She (worked) during the day in a hair salon, and at night she (cooked) for people. She always (thought) about her children. When I (met) her five years ago, she (was) always happy and enthusiastic. I (did not know) her life was difficult. She (told) me that she (did not want) to <u>show</u> her true feelings. Now she <u>is</u> very happy because her children <u>are</u> here, and her life <u>is</u> good.

Writing Task

1 Write page 53

Answers will vary.

2 Self-Edit page 53

Answers will vary.

5 Simple Past, Time Clauses, *Used To*, and *Would*
Science and Society

1 Grammar in the Real World

A page 54

Answers will vary; Possible answer: Ice cream today has more air, which makes the ice cream bigger, softer, less expensive, and longer lasting.

B Comprehension Check page 55

1. noodles   3. France
2. fruit   4. lasted longer

C Notice page 55

1. <u>Before</u> refrigeration existed, (people needed ice to make frozen desserts.)
2. <u>After</u> (scientists found better processes for freezing things,) ice cream became popular with all classes, richer or poor.
3. <u>As soon as</u> (ice cream became more available,) people began to buy it more often.

2 Time Clauses and the Order of Past Events
Exercise 2.1 Time Clauses page 56

2. (Hamwi was a waffle seller at the 1904 World's Fair¹) (when he invented the ice cream cone²).
3. (When an ice-cream seller at the fair ran out of dishes¹) (Hamwi rolled up a waffle²).
4. (The warm waffle turned hard²) (when Hamwi filled it with ice cream¹).

5. (As soon as they saw Hamwi's cones¹,) (all the other ice cream sellers started using them²).
6. (Before Hamwi started an ice cream cone business²,) (he returned from the fair¹).
7. (After Hamwi's story became popular¹,) (many people said that *they* invented the ice cream cone²).
8. (Another man, Italo Marchiony, invented an edible ice cream *cup*¹) (before Hamwi invented his cone²).

Exercise 2.2 Time Words page 57

2. Until   6. until
3. After   7. Before
4. Before   8. As soon as
5. when

Exercise 2.3 Answering Questions with Time Clauses

A page 57

2. f   3. e   4. b   5. c   6. g   7. a

B page 58

Same as **A.**

Exercise 2.4 More Time Clauses

A page 58

Possible answers:
2. As soon as cheap air travel became possible, people started to fly more.
3. Until everyone had a cell phone, people made calls from pay phones.
4. People paid for things with cash or checks before credit cards became popular.
5. Before free education was available, most people did not read or write.
6. When traffic lights came into our cities, roads became safer.
7. After Ford made the first mass-produced car, millions of people learned to drive.
8. Before the first supermarket opened, people bought food from small local stores.

B Pair Work page 58

Answers will vary.

C Over to You page 58

Answers will vary.

3 Past with *Used To* and *Would*

Exercise 3.1 *Used To:* Statements and Questions

A pages 62–63

2. used to listen
3. did; use to spend
4. used to play
5. used to play
6. used to have
7. didn't use to have
8. used to work
9. used to write
10. used to take
11. Did; use to type
12. used to write
13. used to get

B page 63

Answers will vary.

Exercise 3.2 *Would, Used To,* or Simple Past? pages 63–64

3. would burn *OR* burned *OR* used to burn
4. made *OR* used to make *OR* would make
5. didn't / did not travel *OR* didn't use to / did not use to
6. visited *OR* used to visit *OR* would visit
7. didn't / did not used to think *OR* didn't / did not think
8. didn't used to think *OR* thought
9. were *OR* used to be
10. believed *OR* used to believe
11. preferred
12. would make *OR* made
13. changed *OR* would change

Exercise 3.3 *Would:* Questions and Statements

A page 64

Possible answers:
2. Before electricity, how would you light your house?
3. Before electricity, how would you clean your house?
4. Before electricity, what would you do in the evenings?
5. Before electricity, what would you play with?
6. Before electricity, how would you get to work or school?
7. *Answers will vary.*
8. *Answers will vary.*

B Over to You page 64

Answers will vary.

C Group Work page 64

Answers will vary.

4 Avoid Common Mistakes

Editing Task page 65

How did people ~~used~~ *use* to wash dishes? People did not ~~used~~ *use* to have dishwashers before ^*they* invented electricity, so they would wash dishes by hand. But did men and women ~~used~~ *use* to share the dishwashing equally? Not usually. Mostly it was women who did it. Before there was electricity, women ~~use~~ *use* to heat up water on the stove and use it for washing dishes. It took hours and hours, and dishes often broke or chipped.

In 1886, one woman finally got tired of washing dishes by hand. "If nobody else is going to invent a dishwashing machine," she said, "I'll do it myself." Her name was Josephine Cochrane, a housewife and engineer's daughter who was tired of washing – and sometimes breaking – her favorite dishes after dinner parties. Cochrane worked and worked on her invention until 1893 when ^*she* finally created a machine that washed dishes. She showed the machine at the World's Fair that year. People operated it by hand, so it was still hard work. After the fair ended, she started accompany to make the machines. When ^*she* first tried to sell dishwashers, only restaurants and hotels bought them from her. However, after electricity became more easily available, her company built electric dishwashers for people to use in their homes. Today, homes around the world have electric dishwashers.

5 Grammar for Writing
Using Past with *Used To* and *Would*

Pre-writing Task

1–2 page 66

Because of cell phones, our lives <u>are</u> very different than they <u>used</u> to be. Today, (when we <u>want</u> to talk to someone), we can <u>call</u> them anytime. (Before we <u>had</u> cell phones), however, we <u>had</u> to wait (until we <u>were</u> at home). In addition, (before there <u>were</u> cell phones,) we <u>did</u> not know who <u>called</u> us. Now, we always <u>know</u> because cell phones <u>show</u> the caller's number or name. Another change <u>is</u> that parents expect to be in contact with their children more often. (Before I <u>had</u> a cell phone), my parents <u>would</u> not call me very frequently. (After I <u>purchased one</u>), they <u>used</u> to call me many times a day. They <u>would</u> always ask me, "Where <u>are</u> you?" Sometimes, I <u>would</u> not answer my phone. This <u>used</u> to make my parents very angry! They <u>would</u> threaten to take the phone away, but they never <u>did</u>. I <u>am</u> very glad that things <u>are</u> different today, but cell phones <u>do</u> not <u>make</u> everything easier.

1 Write page 67

Answers will vary.

2 Self-Edit page 67

Answers will vary.

6 Past Progressive
Memorable Events

1 Grammar in the Real World

A page 68

Answers will vary; Possible answer: On New Year's Eve, 1999, Emily was watching TV with her family; Steve was in Times Square in New York City; and Bao was working.

B Comprehension Check page 69

Possible answers:

1. Some people were worrying about the Y2K bug.
2. People were attending a concert at the pyramids.
3. Over 2 million people were standing in Times Square.
4. Bao was working because he had a job as a computer technician.

C Notice page 69

1. was watching
2. were standing
3. was sitting

The sentences show an action that was in progress in the past.

2 Past Progressive
Exercise 2.1 Statements and Questions

A page 71

3. was having	12. Were; doing
4. were; celebrating	13. was driving
5. were celebrating	14. were moving
6. were; doing	15. were starting
7. wasn't / was not having	16. was driving
8. was sleeping	17. was
9. were; sleeping	18. were not feeling
10. was working	19. were feeling
11. was having	

B Group Work page 72

Answers will vary.

Exercise 2.2 Time Expressions

A Over to You page 72

2. in; *Answers will vary.*
3. on; *Answers will vary.*

4. at; *Answers will vary.*
5. last; *Answers will vary.*
6. in; *Answers will vary.*
7. in; *Answers will vary.*
8. at; *Answers will vary.*

B Pair Work page 72

Answers will vary.

Exercise 2.3 More Statements and Questions

A page 73

Name	Day / Time	What he or she was doing	How he or she was feeling or thinking
1. Wei	April 25, 2005	1. starting school in the United States 2. studying English for the first time	1. feeling nervous 2. feeling hopeful
2. Nick	June 3, 2009	1. getting his driver's license	1. feeling very excited
3. Ana	the spring of 1999	1. leaving home 2. coming to the United States	1. thinking about her family 2. missing them

B Pair Work page 73

Answers will vary.

C Over to You page 73

Answers will vary.

3 Using *When* and *While* with Past Progressive
Exercise 3.1 Past Progressive or Simple Past?
pages 74–75

2. was traveling	8. was walking
3. was reading	9. saw
4. saw	10. were waiting
5. decided	11. decided
6. said	12. started
7. arrived	13. was happening

Exercise 3.2 Time Clauses page 75

2. When the millennium ~~arrived. Bao~~ *arrived, Bao* was working for a computer company

3. When the power went out‸'we were riding home on the subway.

4. While we were standing in a doorway,^ the ground started to shake.

5. When the earthquake hit,^ she was driving across the bridge.

6. Asha was standing in the town ~~square. When~~ *square when* the sky got dark.

7. Rob was ~~shopping. When~~ *shopping when* the lights went out.

8. While we were ~~working. The~~ *working, the* hurricane hit.

Exercise 3.3 More Time Clauses

A pages 75–76

2. hit	10. got
3. were waiting	11. was waiting
4. shouted	12. was making
5. stayed	13. went
6. ate	14. stayed
7. was shaking or shook	15. played
8. was walking	16. was crashing or crashed
9. told	

B page 76

Possible answers:

2. Where was Samir eating when the earthquake hit?
3. What was Samir eating when the earthquake hit?
4. What was Luisa doing when the hurricane hit?
5. Where was Luisa walking when the lifeguard told her to go home?
6. What was her mother doing when Luisa got home?

C Group Work page 76

Answers will vary.

4 Avoid Common Mistakes

Editing Task page 77

Interviewer: Where ~~you were~~ *were you* when *Apollo 11* landed on the moon?

Maria: Well, in the summer of 1969,^ I was 19. I was living in Mexico. On July 20, I was sitting on the beach with an American couple. We ~~was~~ *were* listening to the ~~radio. When~~ *radio when* the speaker ~~was announcing~~ *announced* the landing.

Interviewer: What ~~you were~~ *were you* doing when the astronauts landed on the moon?

Tom: At that time, my wife and I ~~moved~~ *were moving* from Chicago to San Diego. To save money, we stayed in campgrounds every night. We *were listening* ~~listened~~ to the car radio at our campsite when the astronauts stepped on the moon. That night, while we ~~was~~ *were* lying on the ground,^ we looked up at the moon. We were ~~being~~ amazed!

5 Grammar for Writing

Using Past Progressive and Simple Past Together

Pre-writing Task

1–2 page 78

I <u>was living</u> in Chicago <u>when</u> I (met) my husband. We <u>were</u> both <u>taking</u> classes at the community college there. We (were) not in many classes together, but we <u>were</u> both <u>taking</u> the same math class. I <u>was</u> also <u>working</u> at a coffee shop near the college. One day, my husband (walked) in <u>when</u> I <u>was working</u>. I (recognized) him from our class, but we (did) not know each other's names. We (said) "Hi," but we (did) not say anything else. After that, he (came) in every day. Then, a few weeks later, I <u>was walking</u> out of class <u>when</u> he (asked) me for help with his homework. <u>While</u> I <u>was helping</u> him, we (realized) that we (liked) each other.

Verb form after while: past progressive

Writing Task

1 Write page 79

Answers will vary.

2 Self-Edit page 79

Answers will vary.

7 Count and Noncount Nouns
Privacy Matters

1 Grammar in the Real World

A page 80

Answers will vary; Possible answer: You can protect your personal information by shredding bills and documents with personal information, by only shopping online at well-known sites; and by never answering unsolicited e-mail.

B Comprehension Check page 81

1. c   2. a   3. b

C Notice page 81

2. X   3. X   4. an   5. a
Count: e-mail, bank, papers
Cannot count: permission, information
Plural: papers

2 Count Nouns and Noncount Nouns

Exercise 2.1 Count or Noncount?

A page 83

Noun	Count	Noncount	Plural Form
2. document	✓		documents
3. information		✓	
4. research		✓	
5. equipment		✓	
6. computer	✓		computers
7. software		✓	
8. credit card	✓		credit cards
9. identity	✓		identities
10. safety		✓	
11. privacy		✓	
12. e-mail	✓	✓	e-mails

B pages 83–84

3. X   4. X   5. X   6. X   7. -*s*   8. X
9. -*s*   10. -*s*   11. X   12. X   13. -*s*   14. X

C Pair Work page 84

Answers will vary.

Exercise 2.2 Count and Noncount Meanings page 84

2. experience; NC   6. crimes; C
3. papers; C   7. Life; NC
4. paper, NC   8. lives; C
5. crime; NC

Exercise 2.3 More Noncount Nouns

A page 85

Department	Shop for . . .
Furniture	desks, sofas, tables
Clothes	jeans, shirts, sweaters
Entertainment	CDs, computer games, movies
Sports Equipment	basketballs, soccer balls, tennis rackets
Luggage	backpacks, briefcases, suitcases

B Pair Work page 85

Answers will vary.

Exercise 2.4 Common Noncount Nouns

A pages 85–86

2. airports   6. people
3. publicity   7. travelers
4. evidence   8. traffic
5. progress   9. fun

B Group Work page 86

Answers will vary.

3 Noncount Nouns: Determiners and Measurement Words

Exercise 3.1 Determiners and *Too* and *Enough*

A page 89

2. A lot of   7. any
3. a lot of   8. any
4. some   9. any
5. a lot of   10. not many
6. some

B page 89

2. enough   6. enough
3. Too many   7. too many
4. enough   8. enough
5. too much

Exercise 3.2 Measurement Words

A page 90

2. a   3. d   4. c   5. g   6. e   7. h   8. f

B page 90

2. cartons
3. gallon
4. tube
5. package
6. bar
7. boxes
8. bottles
9. cans
10. pound

C Pair Work page 91

Answers will vary.

D Group Work page 91

Answers will vary.

4 Avoid Common Mistakes

Editing Task pages 91–92

Spyware is ^*a* type of computer software. Someone sends
it to ^*a* computer without your ~~knowledges~~ *knowledge* or ~~permissions~~ *permission*.

It takes control of your computer. It can make your

computer run slowly or even crash. Spyware often records

~~an~~ information about your computer use. It gives the

information to advertisers or other people who want to

collect ~~informations~~ *information* on you. ~~Many~~ *A lot of* spyware sneaks into

your computer when you are downloading and installing

programs from the Internet. One way to prevent ~~a~~ spyware

is to put security settings on your Internet browser. Set

your browser to a medium or higher setting. There is also

~~much~~ *a lot of* software you can buy that blocks spyware.

5 Grammar for Writing
Using Count and Noncount Nouns with Determiners and Measurement Words

Pre-writing Task page 92

Protecting personal (information) is a major problem
today, and it is especially important to protect (details)
like passwords and PINs or personal identification
numbers. Most people have a few PINs and a lot of different
passwords. For example, they use one PIN to get (money)
from the **bank** and another PIN to pay bills by telephone.
In addition, they use **passwords** to get onto websites and
access their (e-mail). One problem is that many people use
the same password for all their accounts and websites.
This is because it is easy to forget different passwords or
PINs. However, this is a bad **idea**. Common (advice) these
days is to have a few passwords and PINs and change them
often. Do not use passwords that are easy to guess, such as
"1234" or your pet's name. Harder passwords make it more
difficult for people to steal your identity.

Writing Task

1 Write page 93

Answers will vary.

2 Self-Edit page 93

Answers will vary.

8 Articles
The Media

1 Grammar in the Real World

A page 94

Answers will vary; Possible answer: People get news online
through social networking sites, e-mail, and customized
news sites.

B Comprehension Check pages 94–95

Possible answers:
1. She checks her phone for news headlines. Then she
   checks a social networking site and her e-mail.
2. The news is becoming an online social activity.
3. People who get the news online leave comments for
   other people to read. They write their reactions to news
   stories on social networking sites and e-mail their
   friends links to interesting stories on news sites.
4. Some popular news subjects are the weather, health,
   business, and international events.

C Notice page 95

1. no; yes
2. no
3. yes; yes

2 Articles

Exercise 2.1 *A* or *An?* page 96

1. A; a   5. a; an
2. a; an   6. a; a; an
3. an; a   7. an; a
4. a; a; an

Exercise 2.2 *A / An* or *The?* page 97

1. b   2. b   3. a   4. b

Exercise 2.3 *A / An, The,* or No Article?

A page 97

2. a   8. ∅
3. an   9. a
4. a   10. A
5. the   11. a
6. the   12. a
7. ∅   13. the

B page 97

Same as **A.**

Exercise 2.4 *The:* Only One or General Knowledge

A pages 98–99

Possible answers:

2. the world	7. The future
3. the media	8. the president
4. The environment	9. the government
5. the sun	10. the public
6. the past	

B Group Work page 99

Answers will vary.

3 Generalizing: More About Articles

Exercise 3.1 Generalizations page 100

2. ∅	10. ∅
3. ∅	11. Most
4. ∅	12. ∅
5. ∅	13. ∅
6. ∅	14. ∅
7. ∅	15. A
8. ∅	16. ∅
9. ∅	

Exercise 3.2 Definitions

A page 100

2. An adult	6. A twenty-something
3. a minor	7. A tween
4. Parents	8. Preteens
5. Seniors	

B Over to You page 101

Answers will vary.

Exercise 3.3 More Generalizations

A page 101

Answers will vary.

B Over to You page 101

Answers will vary.

4 Avoid Common Mistakes

Editing Task page 102

Microblogging is ⟨*a*⟩ way of keeping in touch with other people. ~~The~~ *People* ~~people~~ write microblogs for their friends and families. They use microblogging sites to publish information about their activities. It is an economical way to give a lot of information to a lot of people.

Microblogs are ⟨*a*⟩ very useful method of communicating for companies, too. ~~The companies~~ *Companies* advertise their products with microblogs. They send ~~the~~ information in short messages to customers.

In education, some teachers use microblogging with ~~the~~ students. Students write down all their study activities, and teachers send ~~the~~ advice. Some people use audio blogs in ~~the~~ education. They record ~~the~~ spoken messages and upload them to a microblogging site.

People first started using microblogs in 2005. By 2007, there were 111 microblogging sites around ⟨*the*⟩ world. ~~The~~ ~~microblogs~~ *Microblogs* are becoming more and more popular.

5 Grammar for Writing

Using Articles with Nouns

Pre-writing Task

1–2 page 103

These <u>days</u>, <u>television habits</u> are very different from ⟨the⟩⁴ way they used to be. Many <u>people</u> watch TV <u>shows</u> on⟨the⟩⁵ Internet. Often, you can find <u>a</u>² TV show on⟨the⟩⁵ Internet ⟨the⟩⁴ day after it was on <u>TV</u>. There is <u>an</u>² advertisement about every 10 <u>minutes</u>, but usually there is only one <u>advertisement</u>² at <u>a</u>² time. On <u>TV</u>, there are usually three or more <u>advertisements</u> during <u>a</u>² commercial break. <u>A</u>⁴ commercial break on⟨the⟩⁵ Internet often lasts only 30 <u>seconds</u>. On <u>TV</u>, though, <u>a</u>² commercial break lasts about three <u>minutes</u>. <u>People</u> used to rush <u>home</u> to turn on⟨the⟩¹ television for <u>a</u>² special show, but now they just watch⟨the⟩¹ show online when they are ready. It is like personalized <u>TV viewing</u>.

Writing Task

1 Write page 103

Answers will vary.

2 Self-Edit page 103

Answers will vary.

9 Pronouns; Direct and Indirect Objects

Challenging Ourselves

1 Grammar in the Real World

A page 104

Answers will vary; Possible answer: You will become more confident and more creative, and you will improve your problem-solving skills.

B Comprehension Check page 105

Possible answers:

1. If you challenge yourself, you can be ready to handle tough situations in the future, you will become more confident and more creative, and you will improve your problem-solving skills.
2. Small challenges give people strength to help when they have real problems.
3. 1. Write down your goal and give your plan a start and finish date.
   2. Tell people about your goal.
   3. Go one step further than you originally planned.

C Notice page 105

1. Mari; Mari
2. Ken

2 Pronouns
Exercise 2.1 Pronouns

A page 107

2. myself	10. it
3. myself	11. yours
4. me	12. Ours
5. it	13. our
6. their	14. We
7. yours	15. ourselves
8. herself	16. one another
9. me	17. each other

B Pair Work page 108

Answers will vary.

Exercise 2.2 *One* and *Ones* page 108

2. one	6. ones
3. one	7. one
4. ones	8. one
5. ones	

Exercise 2.3 Prepositions with Reflexive Pronouns

A page 109

2. for	6. about
3. about	7. for
4. to	8. for
5. about	

B Pair Work page 110

Answers will vary.

3 Direct and Indirect Objects
Exercise 3.1 Direct and Indirect Objects

A page 111

2. Mrs. Ramirez gave Vu the names of 10 scholarship organizations.; IO + DO *(IO = Vu; DO = the names of 10 scholarship)*
3. Vu and Mrs. Ramirez sent the completed applications to the scholarship organizations.; DO + PREP + IO *(DO = the completed applications; IO = the scholarship organizations)*
4. A few months later, Vu told Mrs. Ramirez the good news.; IO + DO *(IO = Mrs. Ramirez; DO = the good news)*
5. Five of the 10 organizations offered a scholarship to Vu.; DO + PREP + IO *(DO = a scholarship; IO = Vu)*
6. Vu chose one organization, and it sent a check to his college.; DO + PREP + IO *(DO = a check; IO = college)*

B page 111

2. Mrs. Ramirez gave the names of 10 scholarship organizations to Vu.
3. Vu and Mrs. Ramirez sent the scholarship organizations the completed applications.
4. A few months later, Vu told the good news to Mrs. Ramirez.
5. Five of the 10 organizations offered Vu a scholarship.
6. Vu chose one organization, and it sent his college a check.

Exercise 3.2 *To* and *For* with Direct Objects

A page 112

2. to	3. or	4. for
5. for	6. to	

B Pair Work page 112

Possible answers:
Ken was a biology student at a community college.
Ken argued with the other students a lot.

The exam was about people's ideas and opinions.
It was a free website, and the articles were very interesting.
Ken did very well on the quizzes.
He attended the class regularly and kept notes for Mrs. Green.
Mrs. Green is very proud of him.

Exercise 3.3 Object Pronouns page 113

2. him; She gave an exam to him.
3. him; She found him a critical thinking skills class.
4. him; She wrote a letter of recommendation for him.
5. them; Yes, he e-mailed the applications to them.
6. them; No, it didn't mail them the money.
7. us; No, our school gave a loan to us.
8. you; No, but I can give $50 to you.

4 Avoid Common Mistakes

Editing Task page 114

Lara was afraid of heights. The fear caused many
problems for ~~she~~ *her*. Her life was very difficult. For example,
~~her~~ *she* was very uncomfortable on airplanes. She also did
not like to take elevators in tall buildings. Lara's husband
gave ~~to~~ her some advice. He told ~~to~~ Lara a secret: If she
deals with her fears, she can improve in all areas of her life.
Then her husband found a skydiving class ~~to~~ *for* her. He found
a schedule online, and he gave ~~her it~~ *her the schedule*. Then he gave Lara
money to pay for the class. He also bought the equipment
~~to~~ *for* her. Lara took the class. It was hard, but she challenged
herself. After Lara finished the class, her husband gave
a present ~~for~~ *to* her. He baked ~~for~~ her a cake, and they
celebrated together.

5 Grammar for Writing
Using Pronouns and Objects

Pre-writing Task

1 pages 114–115

Brian and Theresa were happily married, but <u>they</u> never
had enough time for (each other). <u>They</u> were always working
or taking care of (their children). Theresa often worried about
(their relationship), but <u>she</u> never talked to (her husband)
about it. One day, Theresa heard (an interesting program) on
the radio. <u>She</u> told (Brian) about it. The program said that
couples often forgot to have fun with (each other). So <u>they</u>

decided to challenge (themselves) to have more fun together.
That weekend, <u>they</u> went to a local restaurant, and <u>they</u>
did not talk about (their problems). <u>They</u> had (a great time).
After that night, <u>they</u> made (a promise) to (each other). <u>They</u>
promised to do something special together every month.

2 page 115

Reflexive pronoun: themselves
Reciprocal pronoun: each other
Possessive determiners + noun: their children, their
relationship, her husband, their problems

Writing Task

1 Write page 115

Answers will vary.

2 Self-Edit page 115

Answers will vary.

10 Present Perfect
Discoveries

1 Grammar in the Real World

A page 116

Answers will vary; Possible answer: Dr. Smith finds new
medicines in the ocean.

B Comprehension Check page 117

	Did Dr. Smith go there?	Did other scientists go there?	Did people find medicines or chemicals there?
1. the Amazon	☐	☑	☑
2. the Arctic Ocean	☐	☑	☑
3. Africa	☑	☐	☐
4. the Pacific Ocean	☑	☐	☐
5. an underwater volcano	☑	☐	☐

C Notice page 117

1. have discovered
2. 've been
3. 've visited
4. took

We know the exact time the action happened: sentence 4
The exact time is indefinite: sentences 1, 2, 3

2 Present Perfect

Exercise 2.1 Statements page 120

2. have come
3. have gotten
4. have lived
5. haven't / have not received
6. haven't / have not thought
7. haven't / have not taken
8. has taken
9. has developed
10. has set

Exercise 2.2 Questions and Answers

A pages 120–121

2. have; been
3. 've made
4. has gone
5. have; worked
6. 've met
7. have taught
8. 've learned
9. Have; been
10. haven't been
11. has visited
12. 've done

B page 121

1. Central America
2. heart
3. some

Exercise 2.3 More Questions

A pages 121–122

2. Have you lived in Chicago?
3. Where have you traveled?
4. Have you ever visited New York City?
5. Who have you traveled with?
6. How has your family helped you?
7. Has your family given you advice about life?
8. What have you learned in this class?

B Pair Work page 122

Answers will vary.

3 Present Perfect or Simple Past?

Exercise 3.1 Present Perfect or Simple Past?

A page 123

2. grew up
3. studied
4. was
5. joined
6. became
7. has orbited
8. went
9. has studied
10. has seen
11. saw

B Pair Work page 124

1. definite, finished
2. definite, finished
3. definite, finished
4. definite, finished
5. definite, finished
6. definite, finished
7. indefinite, unfinished
8. definite, finished
9. indefinite, unfinished
10. indefinite, unfinished
11. definite, finished

Exercise 3.2 More Present Perfect and Simple Past

A pages 124–125

2. discovered
3. sank
4. have had
5. told
6. was
7. tried
8. felt
9. have seen
10. looked
11. saw
12. hit
13. was

B Over to You page 125

Answers will vary.

4 Avoid Common Mistakes

Editing Task page 126

Claire Smith: How did you decide to become a rain forest explorer?

Bettie Silva: I ~~have been~~ *was* interested in the rain forest when I was a child. I ~~have grown~~ *grew* up in Brazil, and I heard many stories about the rain forest regions in my country as a child.

Claire Smith: When did you go on your first expedition?

Bettie Silva: I ~~have gone~~ *went* on my first expedition in the 1980s. I ~~have seen~~ *saw* a lot of amazing sights on that first trip.

Claire Smith: Where ~~have you gone~~ *did you go* on your first trip?

Bettie Silva: I went to rain forests in the Amazon and in Asia.

Claire Smith: Who ~~you have~~ *have you* traveled with?

Bettie Silva: I've traveled with teams of scientists and other explorers at different times.

Claire Smith: Have you ever had any dangerous experiences in the rain forest?

Bettie Silva: Yes. Sadly, I have ~~loosed~~ *lost* team members. For example, last year, a poisonous snake ~~has bitten~~ *bit* one of my group members. But I *have* ⌃ had many wonderful experiences on trips so far, too. I have helped scientists discover new medicines, and I have ~~meeted~~ *met* many interesting local people.

5 Grammar for Writing

Using Present Perfect and Simple Past Together

Pre-writing Task

1 page 127

Things the writer has done recently: took a trip to Rivertown; has been to the aquarium; has gone to the park

2 page 127

    I do not have time to take long trips, but my family and I (have visited) some interesting places this year. We (have taken) three trips to Rivertown. We <u>went</u> last weekend by car. My sister lives there. We <u>went</u> fishing and <u>had</u> a picnic. We (have been) to the aquarium twice. We <u>went</u> there two months ago by bus. We <u>took</u> a tour, and we <u>learned</u> a lot about the animals. My children <u>loved</u> the sea lions. We (have been) to the park many times. Last night there <u>was</u> a concert. We <u>danced</u> and <u>sang</u>. It <u>was</u> a lot of fun. I like to take small trips to nearby places with my family.

Time expressions with the simple past: last weekend, two months ago, last night
Time expressions with the present perfect: this year, twice, many times

Writing Task

1 Write page 127

Answers will vary.

2 Self-Edit page 127

Answers will vary.

11 Adverbs with Present Perfect; *For* and *Since*
Unsolved Mysteries

1 Grammar in the Real World

A page 128

Answers will vary; Possible answer: Some mysteries that science has not yet solved include bird migration, earthquake lights, disappearing bees, and yawning.

B Comprehension Check page 129

Possible answers:

1. Birds have magnetic particles in their brains to help them find their way.
2. Photographs from the 1960s prove the lights exist.
3. Billions of bees have dies since the 1980s.
4. People yawn when they are tired, when they exercise, and when other people yawn.

C Notice page 129

1. no; yes
2. yes
3. no; yes

2 Adverbs with Present Perfect

Exercise 2.1 *Already, Yet,* and *Still*
pages 130–131

	The action has happened.	The action has not happened.
2. have; noticed	✓	☐
3. has; done	✓	☐
4. hasn't / has not proven	☐	✓
5. haven't / have not been	☐	✓
6. have; determined	✓	☐
7. have; used	✓	☐
8. haven't / have not done	☐	✓

Exercise 2.2 More Adverbs

A pages 131–132

2. recently
3. still
4. already
5. already
6. recently
7. yet
8. still

B page 132

Same as **A**.

Exercise 2.3 Position of Adverbs page 132

2. We have ^*already* seen that humans are living longer and longer.
3. However, we ^*still* have not seen many people live beyond the age of 100.
4. So far, humans have not ^*ever* lived past the age of 130.
5. Researchers have ^*just* begun to understand the processes that occur in the body as we age.
6. ^*Recently* OR Scientists have ^*recently* discovered chemicals in the body that tell it to start aging.
7. Many people wonder what we can do to extend our lives, but science has not found the answers ^*yet*.
8. Some say that eating a low-calorie diet can extend life, but science ^*still* has not proven this.

Exercise 2.4 Questions and Answers

A pages 132–133

Possible answers:

2. What planets have we already sent spaceships to?
3. Have people ever found a cure for the common cold?
4. What medicines have researchers recently discovered?
   OR What medicines have researchers discovered recently?
5. Where have people already looked for new medicines?
6. Has anyone figured out why we dream yet?
7. Have any scientists recently been in the news? *OR* Have any scientists been in the news recently?
8. Have you ever wondered about a scientific mystery?

B Group Work page 133

Answers will vary.

3 Present Perfect with *For* and *Since*

Exercise 3.1 *For* or *Since*?

A page 134

2. for	6. since
3. since	7. for
4. for	8. for
5. since	9. since

B Pair Work page 134

Answers will vary.

Exercise 3.2 More *For* or *Since*?

A pages 135–136

2. for
3. 've / have been
4. since
5. 've / have worked
6. since
7. have; owned
8. 've / have owned
9. since
10. 've / have learned
11. have; done
12. for
13. haven't / have not done
14. haven't / have not eaten
15. since
16. 've / have gotten
17. for
18. haven't / have not exercised
19. for

B page 136

Well, I've lived in California ⟨for⟩ 50 years, and I have been in San Miguel since 1972.

I have not exercised ~~for~~ *in* a long time, but my work is very active.

C Pair Work page 136

Answers will vary.

4 Avoid Common Mistakes

Editing Task page 137

Max is a drama major. Today, he is presenting a scene from a play in one of his classes. He ~~is taking~~ *has taken* acting classes since he was a child. He ~~is acting~~ *has acted* in front of people ~~since~~ *for* many years, and he has been in the drama department ~~since~~ *for* three years. He has ~~ever~~ *never* felt uncomfortable on the stage. However, for some reason, Max ~~just has~~ *has just* forgotten his lines, and his face has become red. Max is blushing.

Many people blush when they are embarrassed, but science has not ~~never~~ *ever* been able to explain why we blush. Researchers know how we blush: The nervous system causes the blood vessels in our face to dilate. This increases blood flow to the face, and this makes it look red. Researchers ~~know~~ *have known* for many years that teenagers blush more than adults do, but ~~still there~~ *there still* has not been much research on blushing.

5 Grammar for Writing

Using Present Perfect with Adverbs and *For* and *Since*

Pre-writing Task

1–2 pages 138–139

There is an area in the woods near my house with a lot of butterflies. Butterflies stop and rest there during their migration south every year. The county bought this land so no one could build houses on it. It has owned the land ⟨for⟩ about eight years. There have been fences around the area ⟨since⟩ 2005 because a lot of people come to see the butterflies.

The number of butterflies that stop at the migration area has decreased every year for the last few years. Scientists have not ⟨yet⟩ learned why. The county has ⟨recently⟩ decided that the butterflies need more protection. They are asking volunteers to stay there during the migration period. Many people have ⟨already⟩ signed up to help.

Adverbs with actions or events that have happened: recently, already

Adverbs with actions or events that have not happened: yet

1 Write page 139

Answers will vary.

2 Self-Edit page 139

Answers will vary.

12 Present Perfect Progressive
Cities

1 Grammar in the Real World

A pages 140–141

Answers will vary; Possible answer: City life is improving through "green" buildings and green belts

B Comprehension Check page 141

Possible answers:

1. People migrate to cities in search of jobs and a better life.
2. When cities grow too fast, there often isn't enough housing for all the new people. Environmental problems get worse, too.
3. Architects and urban planners have found solutions. Architects have designed "green" buildings. Urban planners have been creating green belts in cities.
4. Some green buildings use solar power and less water. In Seoul, South Korea, planners uncovered a small river in the middle of the city and built a park on both sides of the river.

C Notice page 141

1. Environmental problems have been getting worse, too.
2. In addition, urban planners have been creating green belts in cities.

2 Present Perfect Progressive

Exercise 2.1 Statements pages 143–144

2. have been noticing
3. has been picking
4. hasn't / has not been leaving
5. have been feeling
6. have been patrolling
7. has been improving
8. haven't / have not been complaining
9. have been staying
10. have been using

Exercise 2.2 Questions and Answers

A pages 144–145

3. have; been working
4. for
5. has; been focusing
6. since
7. Has; been developing
8. since
9. Have; been addressing
10. for
11. has been happening
12. since
13. since

B Pair Work page 145

Answers will vary.

3 Present Perfect Progressive or Present Perfect?

Exercise 3.1 Present Perfect Progressive or Present Perfect?

A page 147

1. ☑
2. ☐
3. ☐
4. ☑
5. ☑
6. ☑
7. ☐
8. ☐

B Pair Work page 148

Answers will vary.

1. Environmental problems in our city have been increasing.
4. Studies have been showing that green belts have been reducing air pollution.
5. Planners have been talking about creating more green belts in our city.
6. They've / They have been studying the effects of green belts in other cities for the past year.

Exercise 3.2 Present Perfect, Present Perfect Progressive, or Both?

A page 148

2. have opened
3. has been building
4. have; built
5. have moved
6. have been getting / have gotten
7. have closed
8. have gone
9. has been increasing / has increased
10. have broken

B page 148

2. have opened
3. has been building
4. have; built
5. have moved
6. have been getting
7. have closed
8. have gone
9. has been increasing
10. have broken

Verbs you can use both present perfect progressive and present perfect: (6) get, (9) increase

C Pair Work page 148

Answers will vary.

4 Avoid Common Mistakes

Editing Task page 149

Kyle Jones: Urban planners and architects ^*have* been

remodeling city buildings to make them

more energy efficient. This ^*has* been making

life in our city kinder to the environment. It

~~have~~ *has* also been making life healthier for city

residents. Today, we are asking the architect

Vinh Hu about his work. Mr. Hu, how

long ^*have* you been designing green buildings?

Vinh Hu: Oh, a long time. ~~We're~~ *We've / We have been* designing these

buildings for almost 20 years. We've ~~been~~ *believed*

~~believing~~ for a long time that green buildings

are an important way to improve city life.

We've also ~~been knowing~~ *known* for a long time that

most people prefer green apartments. In the

future, no one will want to live in a building

that isn't environmentally friendly.

Kyle Jones: What ^*have* you been working on lately?

Vinh Hu: We've been building two new apartments on

Murray Street.

Kyle Jones: Yes, I ~~am~~ *have been* watching those apartments go up

for a while. What makes them green?

Vinh Hu: They use solar energy for heat.

Kyle Jones: Very interesting! Thank you, Mr. Hu.

5 Grammar for Writing

Using Present Perfect Progressive and Present Perfect Together

Pre-writing Task

1 page 150

Home developers have built 10 new houses in the last two years.

2 page 150

There <u>have been</u> many changes in our neighborhood recently. Home developers <u>have built</u> about 10 new houses in the last two years. This <u>has caused</u> a lot more traffic on our street, and some of our new neighbors (have been driving) too fast through our neighborhood. We (have been trying) to slow them down with signs. We (have) also (been telling) our children not to play soccer and basketball in the street the way they used to. One good thing about this is that the home developer <u>has started</u> construction on a new park nearby. They (have been working) on it for about a month. They <u>have</u> already <u>put</u> in a playground, and there are plans for a skateboard park, as well. We are all looking forward to using it.

How many times something happened: Home developers <u>have built</u> about 10 new houses in the last two years.
An action that is finished: They <u>have</u> already <u>put</u> in a playground.
Use stative verbs: There <u>have been</u> many changes in our neighborhood recently.

Writing Task

1 Write page 151

Answers will vary.

2 Self-Edit page 151

Answers will vary.

13 Adjectives
A Good Workplace

1 Grammar in the Real World

A page 152

Answers will vary; Possible answer: Workers have the right to safe conditions and to fair treatment in the workplace.

B Comprehension Check page 153

Possible answers:

1. Some employers are not ethical, so you should know you rights on the job.
2. Women and men have the right to equal pay for the same job. You also have a right to a workplace that is not hostile.
3. You have the right to free training courses on the safety issues in your workplace. Your company cannot fire you for reporting dangerous or unsafe conditions.
4. You report unsafe conditions to the Occupational Safety and Heath Administration (OSHA).

C Notice page 153

1. Ethical
2. fair
3. hostile
4. embarrassed; humiliated

Words described: employers, treatment, workplace, feel

2 Adjectives

Exercise 2.1 Word Order

A page 154

2. are low
3. are bad
4. are long

B page 155

2. ethical bosses
6. free training courses
7. an eight-hour work day

Exercise 2.2 Using Adjectives

A page 155

2. long
3. fantastic
4. interesting
5. great
6. ugly
7. cotton
8. sport
9. black
10. beige
11. Running
12. Leather

B page 156

Possible answers:

2. two-week
3. three-day
4. black; cotton
5. beige; sport
6. black; leather

Exercise 2.3 Adjective Endings

A page 156

2. -ful
3. -able
4. -ic
5. -ive
6. -ive
7. -ial
8. -ous
9. -ical
10. -ous

B Pair Work page 157

Answers will vary.

3 More About Adjectives

Exercise 3.1 -ed or -ing?

A page 158

1. embarrassed; annoying
2. interested; boring; fascinating; bored

3. annoyed; surprised; depressing
4. relaxing; relaxing; exciting
5. embarrassing; embarrassing

B Pair Work page 158

Answers will vary.

Exercise 3.2 Adjective Patterns

A page 159

2. less friendly ones
3. boring ones
4. older ones
5. unfair one

Exercise 3.3 Adjective Patterns

A page 159

2. However, many ~~aware~~ people are not *aware* of size and age discrimination in the workplace.
3. For example, if a thin woman and an overweight women applyfor the same job, the thin *one* often gets the job.
4. If a tall man and a short man try to get a promotion, the tall *one* often gets the promotion.
5. A recent survey showed that the average Chief Executive Officer (CEO) in the United States is 6 ~~tall~~ feet *tall*.
6. Another survey showed that only 3 percent of CEOs in the United States are less than ~~tall~~ 5 feet, 7 inches *tall*.
7. Many older ~~afraid~~ workers are *afraid* of age discrimination.
8. An older employee with a lot of experience can make ~~nervous~~ a young boss *nervous*.
9. Some laws make ~~illegal~~ age discrimination *illegal*.
10. For example, after you are 40 years *old*, a law called the Age Discrimination Employment Act protects you.

B Pair Work page 160

Answers will vary.

Exercise 3.4 Adjectives After Pronouns

A page 160

Answers will vary.

B Group Work page 160

Answers will vary.

Exercise 3.5 Using *Make* + Object + Adjective

A page 160

Answers will vary.

B Pair Work page 160

Answers will vary.

4 Avoid Common Mistakes

Editing Task page 161

I have a very busy life. I have a fun job, and I am ~~interest~~ *interested*

in my work. My boss is fair, and I work for an ethical

company. I have friends. My life sounds perfect, right?

However, I work a ~~60-hours~~ *60-hour* week. I can't get all my work

done during the day, so I take it home. I do not spend much

time with my husband and our ~~little beautiful~~ *beautiful little* four-~~years~~ *year*-

old daughter. I also do not see my ~~wonderfull~~ *wonderful* friends. This

makes me feel very ~~stress~~ *stressed*. I am never ~~relax~~ *relaxed*. I know my

friends and family are ~~worry~~ *worried* about me.

I think I have a problem. I need some balance between

my work life and my personal life. I know there are ~~usefull~~ *useful*

articles with tips for balancing your life. The problem is, I

do not have the time to read them!

5 Grammar for Writing
Using Adjectives to Describe People, Places, Things, and Ideas

Pre-writing Task

1 page 162

Possible answers:
The writer liked that the workers were very friendly.
The writer didn't like the boss, the low pay, and the awful
smell of the fried food.

2 page 162

I used to work in a <u>fast-food</u> restaurant. There were
some <u>enjoyable</u> things about the job, but there were also
some <u>annoying</u> things about it. We had a <u>terrible</u> boss, but
all the workers were very <u>friendly</u>. We were mostly <u>17-year-
old</u> <u>high school</u> students, so we had a lot of <u>good</u> times
together. We used to tell each other <u>funny</u> or <u>silly</u> jokes all
the time. The boss was the <u>main</u> problem at that job. He
often yelled at us, and that made us all <u>nervous</u>. It made the
customers <u>uncomfortable</u>, too. Also, the pay was <u>low</u>. After
a while, the <u>fried</u> food began to smell <u>awful</u> to us. I was very
<u>happy</u> when I left that job.
Adjectives before nouns: fast-food, enjoyable, annoying,
terrible, 17-year-old, high school, good, funny, silly, main, fried
Nouns used as adjectives: fast-food, 17-year-old, high school
Follow make + object or linking verb: nervous, uncomfortable,
low, awful, happy

Writing Task

1 Write page 163

Answers will vary.

2 Self-Edit page 163

Answers will vary.

14 Adverbs of Manner and Degree
Learn Quickly!

1 Grammar in the Real World

A page 164

Answers will vary; Possible answer: Some ways to learn
a language include listening carefully and taking notes,
making a list of new words and studying them, not
studying for a test at the last minute, not staying up late the
night before a test, and talking to people.

B Comprehension Check page 165

Possible answers:
1. A learning strategy is a technique that helps you learn.
2. Listen carefully and take notes. Also, make a list of new
   words and study the list regularly.
3. A good night's sleep helps you think clearly.
4. Politely ask a person to speak slowly and clearly. If you
   do not understand a word or phrase, politely ask the
   person to explain.

C Notice page 165

1. carefully   3. late
2. regularly   4. politely
The words describe how an action happens.

2 Adverbs of Manner
Exercise 2.1 Forming Adverbs pages 166–167

2. carefully   7. early
3. regularly   8. clearly
4. well   9. well
5. alone   10. quickly
6. hard   11. slowly

Exercise 2.2 Adverb or Adjective? page 167

I'm learning English, and memorization is **hard** for
me. I've heard that some people learn languages (quickly)
because they use *mnemonics*. Mnemonics are memory
tricks. They're **good** for memorizing vocabulary.

The word *mnemonics* looks **strange**. The spelling is **unusual**.
It seems **hard** to pronounce, too. But you can say it (right) if
you forget about the *m* at the beginning – "nuh-mon-iks."

Why is there a silent *m* at the beginning? I don't know. Sometimes English spelling is **silly** like that.

There's a **friendly** vocabulary study group at our Student Learning Center, but I like to study alone. In fact, I easily found two or three great tricks on a website. Here's one: Link new words with words you already know. Take the word *memory,* for example. You can link *memory* with *remember* in your head. Another trick is to find an **easy** rhyme for a word that looks **hard**, like the word *guess.* It sounds like *mess* or *dress.* If you need a **new** strategy that works well, try mnemonics. And let me know if you can find a rhyme for *mnemonics*!

Exercise 2.3 Adverbs and Adjective   page 168

1. well; poorly
2. good
3. late
4. nervous
5. carefully; soundly
6. peacefully
7. properly
8. frequently

Exercise 2.4 Word Order

A page 168

Possible answers:

2. Max is taking notes neatly. *OR* Max is neatly taking notes.
3. Tim always studies alone.
4. She asks questions politely in class. *OR* She politely asks questions in class.
5. My teacher pronounces new words clearly. *OR* My teacher clearly pronounces new words clearly.
6. I study hard, so I pass all my tests easily! *OR* I study hard, so I easily pass all my tests!
7. Ana has learned some mnemonics quickly. *OR* Ana has quickly learned some mnemonics.
8. I proofread my paper carefully. *OR* I carefully proofread my paper.

B Over to You page 168

Answers will vary.

3 Adverbs of Degree

Exercise 3.1 Adverbs of Degree

A page 170

2. really
3. kind of
4. pretty
5. somewhat
6. very
7. very
8. so
9. fairly
10. pretty

B Over to You page 170

Answers will vary.

Exercise 3.2 Using *Too* and *Enough*

A page 171

1. f; hard enough
2. g; too short
3. d; too late
4. h; good enough
5. c; too early
6. b; long enough
7. e; loudly enough
8. a; long enough

B Pair Work page 171

Answers will vary.

Exercise 3.3 Formal Adverbs of Degree
pages 171–172

2. fairly
3. very
4. extremely
5. rather
6. quite
7. extremely
8. very
9. very

Exercise 3.4 Listening for Adverbs of Degree

A pages 172–173

2. pretty
3. so
4. amazingly
5. really
6. kind of
7. really
8. incredibly
9. so

B Group Work page 173

Answers will vary.

4 Avoid Common Mistakes

Editing Task page 174

Marisa: I didn't do ~~good~~ *well* on the test today!

Sam: Did you study ~~hardly~~ *hard* last night?

Marisa: I tried, but it was so loud in the library. How about you?

Sam: I didn't do ~~good~~ *well*, either. I studied, but I didn't sleep ~~pretty~~ *very* well.

Marisa: And the test seemed easy.

Sam: But it wasn't. It was too hard!

Marisa: Well, what happened? We took ~~carefully notes~~ *notes carefully*.

Sam: And we listened ~~good~~ *well* in class.

Marisa: Maybe we didn't study ~~careful~~ *carefully* enough.

Sam: I'm suddenly getting nervous!

Marisa: Why?

Sam: Well, we don't have a ~~pretty~~ *very* long time before the next test!

5 Grammar for Writing
Using Adverbs of Manner and Degree

Pre-writing Task

1 page 175

Possible answer: The trick helps the writer learn vocabulary.

2 page 175

It is (extremely) hard to learn new words. My roommates and I have a vocabulary learning trick that works (very) well for us. First, when we hear or see a new word, we <u>quickly</u> write it down in our vocabulary notebooks. Then, each night, we meet <u>briefly</u> to tell each other our new words. One person <u>carefully</u> chooses one of the words for us. Then, the next day, we all try <u>hard</u> to use that word <u>appropriately</u> as many times as possible. By the end of the day, we <u>usually</u> know the word (pretty) well. Each night, we compare the number of times we used the word. Then the winner chooses the word for the next day. This way, we <u>easily</u> learn about seven new words each week. This trick works <u>well</u> for me, and I recommend it to everyone.

Writing Task

1 Write page 175

Answers will vary.

2 Self-Edit page 175

Answers will vary.

15 Prepositions
Food on the Table

1 Grammar in the Real World

A page 176

Answers will vary; Possible answer: Three places that food goes before it reaches are plates are farms, processing plants, and warehouses.

B Comprehension Check page 177

Possible answers:

1. Businesses threw away 48 billion dollars' worth of food. Families threw away around 25 percent of the food they bought. Most of this food was safe to eat.
2. Farmers throw away food that is the wrong size, shape, or color.
3. Processing plants throw away food that they cannot transport or sell.
4. Food banks are groups that distribute food to poor and hungry people.
5. It is better to buy food from local farmers because this food does not go through processing plants, so there is less waste.

C Notice page 177

1. In; in
2. from; to
3. From; to
4. across

Time: in
Place: in
Movement: from, to, across

2 Prepositions of Place and Time
Exercise 2.1 Prepositions of Place and Time

A page 179

2. near
3. During
4. in
5. On
6. After
7. Before
8. on
9. for

B Pair Work pages 179–180

2. To a processing plant.
3. Near Jeff's farm.
4. For three days.
5. In plastic containers.
6. On the supermarket shelf.

Exercise 2.2 Prepositions of Place

A page 180

2. under
3. on
4. in
5. behind
6. at *OR* behind
7. on; in
8. in; on
9. behind

B Over to You page 180

Answers will vary.

3 Prepositions of Direction and Manner
Exercise 3.1 Prepositions of Direction and Movement pages 182–183

2. from
3. across
4. over
5. to
6. into
7. through
8. around

Exercise 3.2 Pronunciation Focus

A page 184

No answers.

B page 185

No answers.

Exercise 3.3 Prepositions of Place, Manner, and Logical Relationships

A pages 184–185

2. in	8. between
3. on	9. into
4. at	10. on
5. with	11. at
6. in	12. as
7. on	

B page 185

Same as **A.**

C Pair Work page 185

Answers will vary.

4 Phrasal Prepositions and Prepositions After Adjectives

Exercise 4.1 Phrasal Prepositions

pages 187–188

2. such
3. well
4. outside
5. Because
6. instead
7. close
8. instead; well

Exercise 4.2 More Phrasal Prepositions

page 188

2. in front of
3. next to OR close to
4. close to OR next to
5. because of
6. as well as
7. out of
8. outside of

Exercise 4.3 Phrasal Prepositions and Adjectives with Prepositions

A page 189

2. about	6. from
3. at	7. to
4. for	8. with
5. of	

B Pair Work page 189

Answers will vary.

5 Avoid Common Mistakes

Editing Task page 190

Meg Handford lives at[*in*] a small town in Oregon. She read about food processing and distribution. She was worried on[*about*] the amount of gas people use to transport food from farms to supermarkets and from supermarkets to homes. She thought it was bad to[*for*] the environment, so she decided to do something about it.

Meg wanted to make things better. She thought, "Maybe people can share shopping trips." So in July 2007, Meg set up Food Pool.

Food Pool is like a car pool. In a car pool, neighbors and colleagues travel to work together in one car instead of two or three. With Food Pool, neighbors go to the supermarket or a farmers' market together. They do this in[*on*] Saturdays or other free days.

Meg started a website. She was surprised at the number of interested people. Soon her inbox was full in[*of*] e-mails. Now there are more than 50 families at[*in*] her area that share the trip to the supermarket. Food Pool has been running since[*for*] five years and is growing every year.

6 Grammar for Writing

Using Prepositions and Phrasal Prepositions

Pre-writing Task

1 pages 190–191

Possible answers:

The writer recommends checking your refrigerator carefully before shopping and only buying what is on your list.

2 page 191

Food waste is a problem <u>for</u> many people. Here are some suggestions to help you waste less food, save money, and become more responsible <u>for</u> your environment. First, plan your shopping. Make sure you are aware <u>of</u> the food <u>in</u> your refrigerator. Examine your refrigerator carefully. There may be food <u>behind</u> the milk or <u>in</u> the vegetable drawer, so be sure you see everything <u>on</u> the shelves. Next, make a shopping list and become familiar <u>with</u> it. When you are <u>at</u> the supermarket, only buy food <u>on</u> your list. The shelves <u>in</u>

front of you may be full of items on sale, but only buy sale items if you really need them. Finally, check each item on your list during your shopping trip. When you are done, go directly to the cash register. If you follow these suggestions, you will be surprised at the benefits. You will save money, you won't need to go to the supermarket as often, and extra food in your refrigerator will not go bad.

Prepositions that show a place: at, behind, in, on
Prepositions that show a time: during
Prepositions that show a direction: to

Writing Task

1 Write page 191

Answers will vary.

2 Self-Edit page 191

Answers will vary.

16 Future (1)
Life Lists

1 Grammar in the Real World

A page 192

Answers will vary; Possible answer: The writer hopes to ride in a hot-air balloon, live in Spain, write a poem, and travel to all 50 states in the United States.

B Comprehension Check page 193

Possible answers:

1. A life list is a list of things that you are going to do before you die, if you can.
2. People should create life lists because life lists help to motivate people and encourage them to try new things.
3. Make a list that reflects the direction you want for your life. Also, understand that it is going to take time to accomplish the tings on your list.

C Notice page 193

1. 'm going to   3. Are; going to
2. 'm going to   4. is going to
The sentences are about the future.

2 *Be Going To,* Present Progressive, and Simple Present for Future Events

Exercise 2.1 *Be Going To:* Statements
page 195

2. is going to create
3. isn't / is not going to miss
4. are going to attend
5. isn't / is not going to achieve
6. 'm / am going to do

7. 'm / am going to take
8. 'm / am going to learn
9. are going to ride
10. aren't / are not going to do

Exercise 2.2 *Be Going To:* Questions

A pages 195–196

2. are; going to work
3. are; going to do
4. Are; going to get
5. are; going to take
6. Is; going to be
7. is going to happen
8. is; going to happen

B page 196

Possible answers:

2. Where is he going to work?
3. What is he going to do?
4. Is he going to learn a lot on the job?
5. Is he going to take a class at the community college?
6. What is he going to take?
7. Does he think the class is going to be hard?
8. Is he going to visit China very soon?

Exercise 2.3 *Be Going To,* Present Progressive, or Simple Present?

A page 197

2. accomplishing	9. leaves
3. 'm riding	10. are; doing
4. 'm taking	11. 'm going
5. 're going to have	12. 'm picking up
6. 's going to be	13. 's staying
7. are; going	14. arrives
8. 're meeting	15. 're going to have

B page 197

Same as **A.**

Exercise 2.4 More *Be Going To,* Present Progressive, or Simple Present?

A page 198

2. 'm moving
3. leave / 'm leaving
4. 'm going to work
5. start / 'm starting
6. 'm going to travel
7. 's going to be
8. 's going to be
9. 're going to have
10. 's going to rain

11. 're going to need
12. 'm traveling / 'm going to travel
13. arrive / 'm arriving
14. 'm staying / 'm going to stay
15. 's going to be

B Pair Work page 198

Answers will vary.

Exercise 2.5 Statements and Questions

A page 199

Answers will vary.

B Pair Work page 199

Answers will vary.

3 Avoid Common Mistakes

Editing Task page 200

Alex: So, Heather, what *are* you and your husband ~~are~~

going to put on your life lists?

Heather: We *are* going to put a lot of things on our list.

We *are* going to do some things together and some

things separately.

Alex: What *is Tom* ~~Tom is~~ going to do?

Heather: Well, Tom is a twin. He and his brother *are* ~~is~~ going

to attend the International Twins Convention.

Alex: I've heard of that. That's right here in Ohio.

Heather: Right. In fact, the convention is this weekend.

They *are* going to drive there on Saturday.

Alex: That's usually an outdoor event, right?

Heather: Yes, and unfortunately, it *is* going to rain this

Saturday.

Alex: Too bad. What *are they* ~~they are~~ going to do?

Heather: The event is going to be inside at a hotel now.

Alex: That's good. I bet they *are* ~~is~~ going to have a great

time this weekend.

4 Grammar for Writing

Using *Be Going To* and Present Progressive Together

Pre-writing Task

1 page 201

Possible answers:

A lot of married couples are not starting families right away. Instead, they are traveling or they are finishing school, looking for jobs, and working to save money.

2 page 201

Today, more and more couples who want to get married (are not starting) families right after the wedding. There are many reasons for this. Some couples (are graduating) from school before they have children. They know they are going to be busy when they have children, so they want to finish school first. Then, after they finish school, many couples (are planning) to look for jobs and work for a year or two to save money. Other couples are going to travel before they settle down. If they (are not having) children right away, they are going to have interesting stories to tell their families later on!

The present progressive verbs describe definite plans. *Going to* + verb describes plans that are not definite.

Writing Task

1 Write page 201

Answers will vary.

2 Self-Edit page 201

Answers will vary.

17 Future (2)
Getting Older

1 Grammar in the Real World

A page 202

Answers will vary; Possible answer: Some of the effects of people living longer include: more people will have illnesses, there will not be enough doctors, there will be less money for programs such as Social Security and Medicare, many older people will not have enough money, people will need to work into their 70s and 80s, but people may be happier.

B Comprehension Check page 203

Possible answers:

1. By the end of the twenty-first century, there will be several million centenarians in the United States, according to the U.S. Census Bureau.

2. More people will have illnesses such as cancer and heart conditions. Also, there will be less money for programs such as Social Security and Medicare. Therefore, many older people will have to work to an older age.
3. Older people tend to be happier than younger people.
4. Older people tend to be happier because they spend more time on their relationships and know themselves better.

C Notice page 203

1. will   3. will
2. will   4. will

We use *will* to talk about the future.

2 Future with *Will*

Exercise 2.1 *Will:* Statements pages 204–205

2. will see
3. will be
4. will need
5. won't / will not retire
6. will work
7. won't / will not do
8. will help; won't / will not cause

Exercise 2.2 *Will:* Questions and Adverbs

A pages 205–206

2. Why will people have
3. Will people live
4. will everyone be
5. What will happen
6. What will happen
7. how will people like me support
8. What other sources of income will people have

B page 206

2. Better medical care will ^*certainly / definitely / undoubtedly* mean a healthier life.
3. A lot of countries will ^*probably / likely* have more centenarians.
4. ^*Maybe / Perhaps OR possibly* People will ^have more long-term illnesses such as cancer and diabetes.
5. Social Security will ^*probably / likely* begin to have serious problems in the future.
6. Social Security payments will ^*probably / likely* be very low.
7. Most people will ^*certainly / definitely / undoubtedly* need other sources of income as they age.
8. ^*Maybe / Perhaps OR* A lot people your age will ^*possibly* work longer.
9. Many will ^*certainly / definitely / undoubtedly* continue to work full-time for many years.

Exercise 2.3 *Will:* Questions, Answers, and Adverbs

A page 207

1. will not   2. will probably

B page 207

2. undoubtedly   5. very likely
3. probably   6. certainly
4. possibly   7. undoubtedly

C Group Work page 207

Answers will vary.

3 Future with *Will, Be Going To,* and Present Progressive

Exercise 3.1 *Will* or Present Progressive? page 209

2. will grow
3. will increase
4. will probably double
5. will need
6. will announce *OR* is announcing
7. will open *OR* is opening
8. is holding *OR* will hold
9. are teaching *OR* will teach

Exercise 3.2 *Will* or *Be Going To*?

A page 210

2. 'm/am not going to retire *OR* won't / will not retire
3. 'm/am going to travel *OR* 'll/will travel
4. 're not / aren't / are not going to have *OR* won't / will not have
5. 'll/will start
6. are; going to do *OR* will; do
7. 'm/am going to
8. 're not / aren't / are not going to like *OR* won't / will not like
9. 'm/am going to change
10. 'll/will change
11. 'll/will drive

B Pair Work page 210

Answers will vary.

Exercise 3.3 Adverbs

A pages 210–211

2. Computers ^*likely / probably* won't have keyboards. We are ^*maybe / perhaps OR possibly* going to use our voices to communicate with them.
3. There will ^*certainly / definitely / undoubtedly* be no ice in the Arctic.

Maybe / Perhaps OR *possibly* · Maybe / Perhaps OR

4. ^People are not going to drive their own cars. Satellites

possibly

    or computers will ^control them.

certainly OR definitely OR undoubtedly

5. Space flight is ^going to be available to anyone.

certainly OR definitely OR undoubtedly

    People will ^take vacations in space.

B Pair Work page 211

Answers will vary.

C Over to You page 211

Answers will vary.

4 Avoid Common Mistakes

Editing Task page 212

Pablo Percy:	A lot of women actors quit around the age of 40 or 50. They say there aren't good parts for older women. What ^*will* ~~would~~ you do in your later years?
Melanie Hinton:	Well, I won't retire and sit at home. I ^*will* work until I'm 90!
Pablo Percy:	But there aren't many good parts for older women. How ~~would~~ *will* ^you find work?
Melanie Hinton:	The entertainment business is changing. In the future, there ^*will* be a lot more older people making movies *and* watching movies. That means there ~~would~~ *will* ^definitely be more parts for older people, including older women, in the future.
Pablo Percy:	Are you sure?
Melanie Hinton:	Absolutely. In fact, I ~~wouldn't~~ *won't / will not* wait for these parts. I will ~~to~~ write my own scripts. I ^*am* going to have a script ready next year.
Pablo Percy:	What is it going to be about?
Melanie Hinton:	I ^*am* going to write a love story about two 80-year-olds.
Pablo Percy:	Sounds wonderful!

5 Grammar for Writing

Using *Will* and *Be Going To* for Predictions

Pre-writing Task

1 page 213

Possible answers:

The writer's parents want to learn new things and travel more. The mother will take literature classes. The father will learn to cook.

2 page 213

My parents (are going to retire) next year. When they retire, their lives <u>will be</u> very different. Of course they <u>will have</u> a lot more free time. Luckily, they <u>will</u> also <u>have</u> enough money to support themselves and try new things. My mother loves reading books, so she <u>will</u> probably <u>take</u> some literature classes. My father <u>will</u> possibly <u>learn</u> to cook. They both love to travel, so I think they (are going to spend) a lot of time traveling and visiting new places. They <u>will</u> probably <u>see</u> their children and grandchildren a lot more than they do now. They definitely <u>won't run out</u> of things to do when they retire.

Verbs that make predictions based on evidence: will probably take, are going to spend

Writing Task

1 Write page 213

Answers will vary.

2 Self-Edit page 213

Answers will vary.

18 Future Time Clauses and Future Conditionals

Learning to Communicate

1 Grammar in the Real World

A page 214

Answers will vary; Possible answer: Humans learn to communicate through a combination of natural, genetic features and their social environments.

B Comprehension Check page 215

Possible answers:

1. A typical American two-year-old child knows about 200 words.
2. They mostly about things around them – where they are and what they are doing at the moment.

3. They learn to speak about things that are not happening right around them – the past, the future, and faraway people and places.
4. They are our natural, genetic features and our social environment.

C Notice page 215

1. (a) Before; (b) will
2. (a) When; (b) will
3. (a) After; (b) will
4. (a) Once; (b) will

The words in the *a* blanks refer to time.
The verbs in the *b* blanks talk about the future.

2 Future Time Clauses

Exercise 2.1 Future Time Clauses page 217

1. starts; will learn
2. will teach; starts
3. goes; will start
4. will learn; starts
5. gets; will learn
6. is; will recognize
7. will read; goes
8. finishes; will know

Exercise 2.2 Time Words page 218

2. Once
3. As soon as
4. When
5. until
6. When
7. after
8. Before

Exercise 2.3 More Future Time Clauses

A pages 218

2. will know; 1,500
3. finishes
4. knows; 2,500
5. reaches; will know; 3,500
6. reads; writes; will apply

B Pair Work page 219

2. finish; *Answers will vary*
3. will get; *Answers will vary*
4. complete; *Answers will vary*

C Group Work page 219

Answers will vary.

3 Future Conditionals; Questions with Time Clauses and Conditional Clauses

Exercise 3.1 Future Conditionals pages 221–222

3. use
4. will learn
5. will use
6. wants
7. learns
8. will; use
9. will make
10. wants
11. wants
12. will; combine
13. does
14. will make
15. wants
16. will make
17. learns
18. will; learn

Exercise 3.2 More Future Conditionals

A Pair Work page 222

1. b   2. c   3. a

Answers will vary.

B page 223

Possible answers:

2. If you have a new development in technology, you will get a new word that describes it.
3. New words will also enter the language if there is a big world event such as a war.
4. If someone uses the new word on the Internet, people will copy it.
5. For example, if you use the word, your social networking friends will use it, too.
6. If a new word or expression becomes popular, a lot of people will use it.
7. If a person on a TV news show says the new word, it will sound important.
8. A new word will appear in the dictionary if a lot of people use it in speaking and in writing.
9. If people stop using the new word or expression, it will die.

C Pair Work page 223

Answers will vary.

Exercise 3.3 Time Clauses and Future Conditionals

A page 224

1. speaks, reads, and writes English well
2. if he gets a certificate
3. will apply for a certificate program at the community college
4. when he finishes the certificate program
5. will feel very proud

B Pair Work page 224

Answers will vary.

4 Avoid Common Mistakes

Editing Task page 225

A team of scientists is doing experiments with crows to test their intelligence. This is what the scientists think will happen:

- When the crows ~~will be~~ *are* thirsty, they will look for water.

- As soon as they ~~will~~ find water, they *will* drink it.

- If there is no water, the crows *will* search for it.

- If they don't get the water easily, the crows *will* think of ways to get it.

    For example, if the water ~~will be~~ *is* in a narrow tube, it will be difficult to reach it. However, the scientists think that the crows will learn the following:

- If they ~~will~~ drop a stone into the tube, the water level will rise.

- If they ~~will~~ drop more stones, the level will rise more.

- The crows *will* drop stones into the tube until the crows reach the water.

- ~~When~~ *If* the experiment is successful, the scientists will prove that crows are intelligent birds.

5 Grammar for Writing

Using Future Time Clauses and Conditional Clauses

Pre-writing Task

1 page 226

Possible answers:

Marie's goal is to be a nurse. Her steps to reach this goal include completing all four levels of her English program, taking science classes at the community college, applying to nursing school, earning her degree, and looking for a job at a hospital.

2 page 226

Marie is studying English at a community college because she wants to get a better job. She is currently working at a restaurant. She likes it, but she wants to be a nurse one day.

Last week, Marie met with a career counselor at school, and they developed a plan of action. First, <u>before she begins a nursing program</u>, she will need to complete all

four levels of her English program. <u>Once she accomplishes this</u>, Marie will begin taking science classes at the community college. (If she does well in these classes), she will apply to nursing school. (If the school accepts her), she will earn a nursing degree in two or three years. <u>Once she earns her degree</u>, she will look for a job at a hospital. (If she completes all of these steps), she will accomplish her goal of becoming a nurse.

Possible answers:

Marie is less sure of doing well in science, of being accepted to nursing school, and of completing all of these steps.

Writing Task

1 Write page 227

Answers will vary.

2 Self-Edit page 227

Answers will vary.

19 Ability
Amazing Science

1 Grammar in the Real World

A page 228

Answers will vary.

B Comprehension Check page 229

2. c   3. a   4. d

C Notice page 229

line 2	can
line 3	can't
line 8	are not able to
line 15	could
line 19	(will be able to)
line 21	can
line 25	can't
line 32	were not able to
line 35	(will be able to)

2 Ability with *Can* and *Could*

Exercise 2.1 *Can* and *Can't*: Statements
page 231

2. can't move
3. can't talk / speak
4. can't breathe
5. can; move
6. can speak / talk
7. can send
8. can use

Exercise 2.2 *Can* and *Can't*: Questions and Answers

A pages 231–232

2. Can they speak?
3. How many languages can they understand?
4. Can they lift patients?
5. How much weight can one robot lift?
6. Can a robot recognize people?
7. Can they give medicine to people?
8. What kinds of decisions can they make?

B page 232

2. They can speak quite well.
3. They can understand eight languages.
4. They can move patients from beds to wheelchairs.
5. They can lift up to 134 pounds.
6. It can recognize patients, doctors, and other nurses.
7. They can't change a patient's medicines.
8. So far they can make very simple decisions.

C page 232

Possible answers:

1. They can't change beds.
2. They can't lift very heavy patients right now.
3. They can't change a patient's medicines.

Exercise 2.3 *Can, Can't, Could,* or *Couldn't?*

A pages 232–233

2. can
3. can
4. can
5. can
6. Can
7. could
8. Can
9. can't
10. can
11. can

B Group Work page 233

Answers will vary.

3 *Be Able To*

Exercise 3.1 Questions and Answers

A page 236

2. Are; able to read
3. Are; able to see
4. were able to prove
5. was able to show
6. will; be able to use
7. are able to tell
8. will be able to use
9. will be able to see
10. will; be able to use

Can use *could*: 5

B Pair Work page 236

Answers will vary.

Exercise 3.2 *Be Able To* After Other Verbs

A Over to You page 237

Answers will vary.

B Group Work page 237

Answers will vary.

4 Avoid Common Mistakes

Editing Task page 238

Will people really need to ^*be* able to speak other languages in the future? That is a question language students ask after they hear about the Instant Interpreter. This little machine translates for you when you visit a foreign country. It listens to what you say and is able ^*to* translate your speech into eight world languages. It is also easy to use. If you are able ^*to* use a smart phone, you will ^*be* able to use this.

I tried the Instant Interpreter last week, and I liked it. I ^*was* able to order a cup of coffee in a restaurant. When the server asked me a question, the Interpreter gave me the translation, and I was able to answer. In the end, we were able to have a simple conversation. However, we ^*were* not able ^*to* understand everything we said to each other.

One problem with this machine is that it ~~can not~~ *cannot* work quickly when your conversation becomes more complex. It needs time to ^*be* able to learn your voice, too. I ~~could~~ *was able to* solve the problem by talking to it a lot, so it learned my voice.

If you need to be able ^*to* get around in a foreign city, this is a good buy. You ~~can not~~ *cannot* find a better translating machine on the market today.

5 Grammar for Writing

Using *Can, Cannot,* and *Be Able To* in the Present and Future

Pre-writing Task

1 page 239

Possible answer:

The writer thinks that in the future, people will be able to listen to music on more advanced digital music players.

These players will be very thin, stick to skin, and charge the batteries on body energy.

2 page 239

Today people <u>can listen</u> to music everywhere they go. When you walk down the street, you <u>can see</u> old and young people using ear buds. Digital music players are essential devices for many people these days, and I think they will become even more convenient in the future.

When I was young, I had a portable CD player. I could take my CD player everywhere, but I had to carry disks and buy batteries. I did not care. I loved my CD player.

Now I have a digital music player. It is much better than my old CD player. I <u>can take</u> it everywhere, and I <u>can download</u> many different kinds of music. In the future, I think digital music players will continue to get better. They will be very thin, and they will stick to the skin. People (will be able to walk around) and not worry about the devices. Also, we will not have to worry about batteries. The energy from our bodies will charge the batteries.

Verbs that talk about the present: can listen, can see, can take, can download
Verbs that talk about the future: will be able to walk around

Writing Task

1 Write page 239

Answers will vary.

2 Self-Edit page 239

Answers will vary.

20 Requests and Offers
Good Causes

1 Grammar in the Real World

A page 240

Answers will vary; Possible answer: Lisa is trying to organize volunteers to serve Thanksgiving dinner at the Bay City Homeless Shelter.

B Comprehension Check page 241

2. e   3. b   4. a   5. c

C Notice page 241

1. could you
2. would you
3. may I
4. can I

Ask permission to do something: sentences 3 and 4
Ask someone else to do something: sentences 1 and 2

2 Permission

Exercise 2.1 Asking and Answering Requests for Permission pages 243–244

2. Hi, Lisa: Do you mind if I ~~picks~~ *pick* up the turkey on Wednesday morning? Thank you, Professor Rodriguez

3. Dear Lara: Ana's oven is not working. Do you mind if she ~~cook~~ *cooks* the turkey at your house? Thanks! Lisa

4. Hello, Lisa: Can my roommate ~~calls~~ *call* you about volunteering? Do you mind if I give him your number? Mohammed

5. Dear Ana: May ~~please I~~ *I please* call you early on Wednesday morning to arrange a time? Professor Rodriguez

6. Dear Lisa: Yes, I can bring plates. Can you ~~helping~~ *help* me carry them? Thanks! Marcus

7. Dear Professor Rodriguez: Yes, ~~may you~~ *you may* call on Wednesday morning. I'm available after 8:00 a.m. Ana

8. Hi, Ana: My car is not working. Could I please ~~to~~ ride to the shelter with you? Eun

Exercise 2.2 Formal Requests for Permission

A–B page 244

	Yes	No
2. Could I leave	✓	☐
3. Do you mind if we use	✓	☐
4. Do you mind if we borrow	✓	☐
5. Do you mind if we give you	✓	☐

C Pair Work page 244

No answers.

Exercise 2.3 Asking for Permission

A pages 244–245

Answers will vary.

B Pair Work page 245

Answers will vary.

C Pair Work page 245

Answers will vary.

3 Requests and Offers

Exercise 3.1 *Can, Could, Will,* and *Would:* Requests and Answers

A pages 247–248

2. Would you please set up tables? *OR* Would you set up tables, please?
3. Can you please sell raffle tickets? *OR* Can you sell raffle tickets, please?
4. Will you please buy prizes for the raffle? *OR* Will you buy prizes for the raffle, please?
5. Would you please decorate the room? *OR* Would you decorate the room, please?
6. Could you please serve snacks and drinks? *OR* Could you serve snacks and drinks, please?
7. Will you please give a speech about the charity? *OR* Will you give a speech about the charity, please?
8. Would everyone please help clean up after the party? *OR* Would everyone help clean up after the party, please?

B Pair Work page 248

Answers will vary.

Exercise 3.2 Formal and Informal Offers and Responses

A pages 248–249

2. we can help you; OK, thanks.
3. Could I help you; No, thank you.
4. Can I put; Yes, please. Thanks!
5. we'll help; OK, thanks.
6. may I help you; Yes, please. Thank you.
7. I can clean it up.; Thanks!
8. Can I finish; Yes, thank you.

B page 249

3 and 6.

Exercise 3.3 Requests and Offers

A Pair Work page 249

Answers will vary.

B Pair Work page 250

Answers will vary.

C Group Work page 250

Answers will vary.

4 Avoid Common Mistakes

Editing Task page 251

Hi, Luis. Do you mind if we change the time to meet at the

park tomorrow? Could we ~~to~~ meet at noon? Peg

Hi, Peg. Yes, we ~~could~~ *can*. I will be there a few minutes before

noon. Do you mind if Omar comes, too? He wants to help. Luis

Hi, Luis. No, that's fine. ~~Please would you ask him to call me?~~ *Would you please ask him to call me? / Would you ask him to call me, please?*

Peg

Hi, Peg. Yes, I ~~would~~ *will*. We'll ~~to~~ bring soda. OK? Luis

Hi, Luis. That would be great. I can ~~to~~ make some

snacks. Oh, could ~~please~~ you *please* bring plates and napkins *please*?

Thanks! Peg

5 Grammar for Writing

Permission, Requests, and Offers in Writing

Pre-writing Task

1 page 252

Possible answers:

Alicia offers to bring sandwiches and her laptop. She needs Yan and Kobe to meet at 1:00 tomorrow. She needs to know if they can meet at Kobe's house, if Kobe could provide soda or juice, could call the homeless shelter, and to let her know if she needs to bring her laptop. She needs Yan to get information on the soup kitchen.

2 page 252

Dear Yan and Kobe,

We need to work on our group project tomorrow. <u>Do you mind if I ask you both to help me with some things?</u> Thanks. Here are the things we need to do.

• <u>Could we all meet at 1:00 tomorrow to work on the project?</u> The only problem is, my roommate is having a study group at the apartment at that time. <u>Kobe, do you mind if we meet at your house instead of my apartment?</u>

• If we meet at Kobe's house, I could bring some sandwiches. <u>Yan, would you be able to bring some dessert? Kobe, could you provide soda or juice?</u>

• <u>Yan, could you get the information on the soup kitchen before we meet?</u>

• <u>Kobe, would you call the homeless shelter and set up an appointment for us to talk to the director?</u>

• <u>Kobe, could you let me know if you want me to bring my laptop?</u>

See you both tomorrow!

Alicia

Writing Task

1 Write page 252

Answers will vary.

2 Self-Edit page 253

Answers will vary.

21 Advice and Suggestions
The Right Job

1 Grammar in the Real World

A page 254

Answers will vary.

B Comprehension Check page 255

1. different things
2. can
3. difficult
4. Not everyone

C Notice page 255

1. ought to
2. should
3. could

Ought to and *should* show advice.
Could makes a suggestion.

2 Advice
Exercise 2.1 Statements page 257

Possible answers:

2. You really had better think about the hours you prefer.
3. Perhaps you ought to decide if you want to be on call 24-7.
4. Maybe you should look for job advertisements online.
5. You probably ought to tell your family about your plans.
6. You really shouldn't get discouraged.
7. I think you should ask for advice from a career counselor.
8. You really had better not take a job you don't like!

Exercise 2.2 Asking for and Giving Advice

A page 258

2. Who should
3. Should
4. What should
5. Should
6. What should
7. Should

B Pair Work page 259

Answers will vary.

C page 259

2. should probably talk
3. Maybe; ought to take
4. Perhaps; should look
5. really ought to do
6. should really start
7. I think; had better start; should probably talk
8. ought to do

Exercise 2.3 More Asking for and Giving Advice

A page 259

Answers will vary.

B Pair Work page 259

Answers will vary.

3 Suggestions
Exercise 3.1 Making Suggestions page 261

2. Why not
3. might want to
4. You might want to
5. we could
6. might not want to
7. You might want to
8. Why don't

Exercise 3.2 More Suggestions

A Pair Work page 262

Answers will vary.

B Over to You page 262

Answers will vary.

4 Avoid Common Mistakes
Editing Task page 263

Jordan: There are a lot of changes happening at my company. I'm worried I might lose my job.

Isabela: Well, you ᴬhad better probably start looking for something else.

Jordan: I guess so.

Isabela: At the same time, you _had_ better try to keep your current job. They say it's a lot harder to find a new job when you're unemployed.

Jordan: Is there anything I can do?

Isabela: Yes, there's a lot you can do. First, why not ~~to~~ talk to your boss? You get along well, right? Why not _ask_ ~~asking~~ for feedback on your work? Then, you probably ought to tell your boss you're working on those things. You might want to keep in touch with her by e-mail.

Jordan: OK. What else?

Isabela: Well, do extra work. You ought to take on extra tasks whenever you can. And you ~~could not~~ _might not want to_ complain about anything.

Jordan: That makes sense. Thanks, Isabela. ~~I'd better~~ _I should_ ask you for advice more often!

5 Grammar for Writing
Giving Advice and Suggestions

Pre-writing Task

1 pages 264–265

Possible answer: Nervous in New York is asking for help with her first job interview next week; _Answers will vary._

2 page 265

Dear Nervous,

Here is some general job-interview advice. Good interviewers ask you questions, but they also want you to ask questions. You should come to the interview with interesting questions. This will help you to feel well prepared. Also, you should be ready to write down some questions during the interview, so you should bring a small notebook. This shows that you are very interested in what the interviewer is saying. You might want to ask the interviewer if it is all right to take notes first, though. Interviewers often ask about your weaknesses. You really should make a list of them in advance. I think you should be honest about your weaknesses, but only the weaknesses that will not cause problems on the job. Also, you had better be ready to talk about your plans to overcome these weaknesses. This shows that you want to learn and grow in your job. In addition, you really ought to practice an interview in advance. Perhaps you could ask a friend to

help you. However, you had better do that a few days in advance so you have time to fix any problems.

If you follow this advice, you show the interviewer that you are serious about the job and the company, and that helps you feel less nervous.

Good luck,

Aunt Advice

The sentences with _really should, had better,_ and _really ought to_ offer strong advise. The words that make the advice strong are _really_ and _had better._

Writing Task

1 Write page 265

Answers will vary.

2 Self-Edit page 265

Answers will vary.

22 Necessity, Prohibition, and Preference
How to Sell It

1 Grammar in the Real World

A page 266

Answers will vary; Possible answer: Difficulties for advertisers: The large amount of choices consumers have, advertising is very expensive, advertisers must follow many rules.

B Comprehension Check page 267

Possible answers:

1. In the past, sellers called out to people on the street and tried to persuade people to buy their products.
2. It is difficult because people have so many choices these days.
3. They see or hear up to 3,000 advertising messages each day.
4. Advertisers must not lie.

C Notice page 267

1. need to
2. would rather
3. would prefer
4. has to

Necessary: sentences 1 and 4
Preferred: sentences 2 and 3

2 Necessity and Prohibition

Exercise 2.1 Statements

A page 269

2. needs to
3. has to
4. need to
5. must
6. must
7. doesn't have to; needs to
8. can't; need to
9. 've got to
10. must

B page 269

Not Necessary: sentence 7
Prohibited: sentence 8

Exercise 2.2 Questions and Answers page 270

2. have to
3. Do; have to
4. don't / do not need to
5. must
6. have to
7. has to
8. needs to
9. does; need to
10. Do; have to
11. have got to
12. needs to

Exercise 2.3 More Questions and Answers

A Over to You page 271

Answers will vary.

B Pair Work page 271

Answers will vary.

C Group Work page 271

Answers will vary.

3 Preference

Exercise 3.1 Questions and Answers
pages 273–274

2. would rather not get
3. prefers to get
4. Would; rather see
5. wouldn't / would not like to see
6. 'd / would rather see
7. Would; prefer to see
8. 'd / would rather not
9. 'd / would prefer to hire

Exercise 3.2 More Questions and Answers

A page 274

2. Do you prefer advertising by mail or e-mail ads? *OR* Do you prefer e-mail ads or advertising by mail?
3. Would you like to see a lot of ads before you buy things?
4. Would you prefer to watch TV without commercials?
5. Would you rather not have advertising online?
6. Do you prefer ads on the radio or ads on TV? *OR* Do you prefer ads on TV or ads on the radio?
7. Would you like to see more informative ads or more funny ads?
8. Would you rather not have any advertising at all?

4 Avoid Common Mistakes

Editing Task page 275

Dear Adam,

I want to check in on our progress. Would you like ~~to~~ do it via e-mail, or would you rather ~~to~~ meet in person? It ~~must~~ *doesn't / does not need / have to* ~~not~~ take long. It would probably only take half an hour, but I *'d / would* rather not wait too long.

– Ingrid

Hello, Ingrid,

Good idea. I would prefer *to* meet in person. We ~~must not~~ *don't / do not need / have to* meet in the office if we don't want to. We could meet at the café on the corner. Where would you rather ~~to~~ meet? And when would you prefer to meet? I am free tomorrow afternoon or Thursday after 4 o'clock.

– Adam

Hi, Adam,

Sam would like to join us, and he would rather ~~to~~ meet on Thursday. How about Thursday at the café at 4:15?

– Ingrid

Hi, Ingrid,

OK! See you then.

– Adam

5 Grammar for Writing

Writing About Necessities and Expressing Preferences

Pre-writing Task

1 page 276

Possible answers:

There are too many e-mail advertisements, it takes too long to delete them, and many are from criminals. The writer thinks people would like an e-mail service that automatically deletes the ads. The writer also says the government needs to do more.

2 page 276

There are too many e-mail advertisements. These e-mails advertise cheap watches, medicine, diet pills, online classes, and other things. <u>Most people do not need to buy these things.</u> (They would prefer not to see ads for them.) <u>They often have to delete 20 or 30 of these e-mails every day.</u> This takes too much time. (Many people would like to use an e-mail service that automatically deletes them. Some people would rather not receive these e-mails, so they send reply e-mails to the ads to unsubscribe to them.) This does not usually help. (In addition, many of these e-mails are from criminals who would like to steal from you.) For example, the e-mail offers a great price on jewelry, but you need to enter your credit card number. The thieves use your credit card to buy things for themselves. <u>Of course, the law says they must not do this, but it is very common.</u> <u>The government needs to do more to stop these criminals.</u>

Writing Task

1 Write page 277

Answers will vary.

2 Self-Edit page 277

Answers will vary.

23 Present and Future Probability

Life Today, Life Tomorrow

1 Grammar in the Real World

A pages 278–279

Answers will vary; Possible answer: In the United States now, the yearly birthrate is declining. This may continue in the future, causing less crowded cities, less pollution, fewer people in the workforce, or a decline in the number of doctors and the quality of health.

B Comprehension Check page 279

Possible answers:

1. Women might be choosing to have fewer children because more women now have careers. The economy might also affect birth rates.
2. Today, it costs more than $300,000 to raise a child from birth to age 17.
3. Cities could become less crowded, and there may be less pollution.
4. There might be fewer people in the workforce. There could be fewer doctors, and this could cause a decline in general health.

C Notice page 279

1. might
2. could
3. could
4. might

Might and *could* describe things that are uncertain. They are used to talk about both the present and the future.

2 Present Probability

Exercise 2.1 Present Probability

A page 281

2. can't	7. can't
3. must	8. could
4. could	9. might
5. may not	10. could
6. might	11. must

B page 282

	Not Certain	Almost Certain
2.	☐	☑
3.	☐	☑
4.	☑	☐
5.	☑	☐
6.	☑	☐
7.	☐	☑
8.	☑	☐
9.	☑	☐
10.	☑	☐
11.	☐	☑

Exercise 2.2 Questions and Answers About Present Probability page 282

2. may be
3. must
4. should
5. might not
6. can't be
7. might
8. may

Exercise 2.3 Using Modals of Present Probability

A Over to You page 283

Answers will vary.

B Pair Work page 283

Answers will vary.

3 Modals of Future Probability

Exercise 3.1 Future Probability

A page 285

2. may
3. could
4. will
5. might not

6. could
7. might not
8. could

B page 285

	Not Certain	Certain
2.	✔	☐
3.	✔	☐
4.	☐	✔
5.	✔	☐
6.	✔	☐
7.	✔	☐
8.	✔	☐

Exercise 3.2 Practicing Future Probability
page 286

2. might
3. might
4. may
5. could
6. might
7. could
8. could
9. may
10. may

Exercise 3.3 Using Modals of Future Probability

A Over to You page 286

Answers will vary.

B Group Work page 287

Answers will vary.

4 Avoid Common Mistakes

Editing Task pages 287–288

Jim: OK. The trend we're going to discuss in our presentation is the increase in the number of people going to college. Let's start by discussing reasons.

Lucy: Well, it ~~can~~ *might* be because a lot of people are unemployed. They ~~can~~ *might / may / could* be getting a degree because they don't have work. They stay busy at school.

Alex: Yes, I think that ~~maybe~~ *may be* the most important reason.

Jim: But is that the only reason?

Lucy: No, it can't *be*.

Alex: ~~May be~~ *Maybe* students are also preparing for a better job.

Lucy: Yes, that ~~can~~ *might / may / could* be another reason.

Jim: OK, good. ~~May be~~ *Maybe* we'll add more reasons later. What about the future effects of this trend, though? Will they be good or bad?

Alex: There ~~must~~ *will* be a lot of good effects in the future, I'm sure. It ~~must~~ *will* be good to have more educated people in the workplace in the future.

Lucy: Yes, but there ~~can~~ *may / might / could* be some problems in the future, too. People could have a lot of debt when they finish school.

Jim: Hmm. Good point. I think it ~~couldn't~~ *may not / might not / shouldn't* be difficult to think of several more effects. We're doing very well so far. Let's summarize our ideas and see if we need any more information. We ~~couldn't~~ *might not / may not* have enough, or we might have just what we need.

5 Grammar for Writing

Writing About Probability in the Present and Future

Pre-writing Task

1 pages 288–289

Possible answers:

The trend of students going to community college and then transferring to universities after two years.

2 page 289

More students are going to community colleges these days. Many of these students are planning to transfer to universities after two years. This trend <u>could</u> be because universities are getting more expensive. They are also becoming more competitive. This <u>could</u> be because more young people want to go to college than before. This <u>must</u> be making the universities harder to get into. It <u>should</u> also make community colleges more competitive in the future. In addition, class sizes <u>might</u> get bigger. Students <u>may not</u> be able to register for the classes they want. It <u>could</u> take longer than two years for a full-time student to finish. The average age of university juniors and seniors <u>could</u> start to rise. However, community colleges are also getting more tuition money. As a result, they <u>should</u> be able to avoid these problems by hiring more teachers in the future.
Present probability: could, must
Future probability: might, may not, could
Certain about the future: should

Writing Task

1 Write page 289

Answers will vary.

2 Self-Edit page 289

Answers will vary.

24 Transitive and Intransitive Verbs; Verbs and Prepositions
Getting Along at Work

1 Grammar in the Real World

A page 290

Answers will vary.

B Comprehension Check page 291

Possible answers:

1. Some people are allergic to perfume.
2. Jorge told a joke that may have offended a co-worker.
3. Humor is very different in different cultures.
4. Mei Lee's boss makes outrageous demands and asks Mei Lee to do personal tasks for her.

C Notice page 291

1. arrived
2. happened
3. told
4. offended

Verbs followed by a noun or pronoun: told, offended

2 Transitive and Intransitive Verbs
Exercise 2.1 Transitive or Intransitive?
page 293

Hi Emily,

Our new assistant started (work) [T] yesterday. He seems [I] great, except for one thing. He chews (gum) [T] all the time. It distracts (me) [T] and the other employees. We hear (it) [T] all day long. Maybe I should explain (my feelings) [T], but I do not want to offend (him) [T]. He works [I] hard and everyone likes (him) [T]. I discussed (the problem) [T] with my co-worker, Kyle, but he didn't care. He just laughed [I]. When I arrived [I] at work this morning, my manager and I spoke [I]. She understood [T] (the problem). She is going to say (something) [T] to the new assistant. Maybe that will help [I].

I hope your workday is going [I] better than mine!

Yvette

Exercise 2.2 Questions and Answers

A page 293

2. How often do you (stay) late at work (or school)?
3. What time do you usually (leave) for work (or school)?
4. What has (changed) in your work (or school) life recently?
5. What time do you usually <u>begin</u> your workday (or school day)?
6. What time does your workday (or school day) usually (end)?

B Pair Work page 294

Answers will vary.

3 Verb + Object + Preposition Combinations
Exercise 3.1 Verb + Object + Preposition Combinations page 295

2. spent; with
3. discussed; with
4. borrowed; from
5. asked; for
6. get; from
7. reminded; about
8. help; with
9. thanked; for

Exercise 3.2 More Verb + Object + Preposition Combinations

A Over to You page 295

Answers will vary.

B Pair Work page 295

Answers will vary.

4 Verb + Preposition Combinations

Exercise 4.1 Verb + Preposition Combinations in Statements page 297

2. talked about
3. listened to
4. think about
5. ask about
6. look at
7. talking to
8. belong to
9. ask for
10. agreed with
11. argued with

Exercise 4.2 Verb + Preposition Combinations in Questions

A page 298

2. What do you usually talk about at work (or school)?
3. What do you worry about at work (or school)?
4. Who do you depend on for help?
5. Whose advice do you listen to most?
6. Who do you sometimes argue with?
7. Who do you usually agree with?
8. What clubs or professional organizations do you belong to?

B Pair Work page 298

Answers will vary.

5 Avoid Common Mistakes

Editing Task page 299

Do these problems sound familiar to you? If so, you are not alone. These are the common problems our readers sent to us in our recent survey. Try our solutions! They could help you change your work life forever!

■ Problem: Some people do not appreciate me, or even like ^me.

Solution: Maybe you should talk ^to your boss about the problem.

■ Problem: My co-workers often argue ^with me. I don't like it.

Solution: You could talk ~~with~~ ^about the problem with your co-workers.

■ Problem: Nobody listens /to me when I have a new idea.

Solution: Maybe you need to explain your ideas more clearly to them.

■ Problem: I always thank my co-workers for their help, but they never thank ^me.

Solution: You could discuss ~~about~~ the problem with them, but this may not change.

■ Problem: My co-worker always asks me ^for help. I don't mind helping him, but then I don't finish my own work.

Solution: Discuss this ^with him. Tell him you want to help, but you must also do your work. I think he'll understand.

6 Grammar for Writing
Using Transitive and Intransitive Verbs

Pre-writing Task

1 page 300

Possible answers:

Choose the right time to ask your boss for a raise. Be prepared to provide reasons why you should get a raise. Be confident when you talk with your boss.

2 page 300

If you are like most people, you (work hard at) your job and you believe you are good at it. You also probably believe that you deserve more money. The problem is, how do you ask your boss for a raise? Here are a few suggestions for this problem. First, choose the right time to ask your boss. Some managers believe their employees should not (ask for) them. Other bosses are happy to discuss salary with their employees, but only when they are in a good mood and are not too busy. You might want to (talk about) this with your co-workers before you ask. Second, before you ask your boss, be prepared. (Think about) things you do to help the company. What do people (depend on) you for? Do you (look for) ways to save money? Make a list of these things so you can remind your boss about them. Finally, when you ask your boss, be confident. Don't (apologize for) your desire to make more money. (Don't worry about) bad things that probably won't happen – for example, your boss is probably not going to (laugh at) you. At the same time, you should also be polite. Explain your opinion to your boss gently, with a smile. Also, don't forget to thank your boss for his or her time.

Writing Task

1 Write page 301

Answers will vary.

2 Self-Edit page 301

Answers will vary.

25 Phrasal Verbs
Money, Money, Money

1 Grammar in the Real World

A page 302

Answers will vary; Possible answer: Step 1 is to figure out your income and your spending habits. Step 2 is to set up a budget.

B Comprehension Check page 303

Possible answers:

1. You should write down your expenses so that you get a clear picture of your usual spending habits.
2. Rent, food, electricity, and gas are the most important expenses.
3. Movies and dinners out are not important expenses.
4. Two goals are paying off your credit card and saving for a large purchase.

C Notice page 303

1. sort out; set in
2. Sit down
3. write down

Words in each blank: two
Transitive words: sort out, write down
Intransitive words: set in, sit down

2 Intransitive Phrasal Verbs

Exercise 2.1 Intransitive Phrasal Verbs
page 305

1. A: Come on! We're going to be late.
   B: Hold on. I'm coming.
2. A: It's Friday night. Let's eat out somewhere.
   B: I can't. My money's already run out, and I don't get paid until next week.
3. A: I have some new neighbors. They moved in last week.
   B: Are they nice? Do you think you'll get along?
4. A: I want to go out now. Do you want to come?
   B: No, go ahead. I'm tired. I'm going to stay home.

Exercise 2.2 Using Phrasal Verbs

A pages 305–306

2. along	8. out
3. away	9. on
4. back	10. up
5. in	11. down
6. out	12. down
7. out	13. on

B Pair Work page 306

Answers will vary.

C Group Work page 306

Answers will vary.

Exercise 2.3 Questions and Answers

A page 306

2. out	5. up
3. out	6. on *OR* ahead
4. down	7. out

B Pair Work page 306

Answers will vary.

3 Transitive Phrasal Verbs

Exercise 3.1 Transitive and Intransitive
Phrasal Verbs page 309

2. Most experts say it's a good idea to **write down** all your expenses. T
3. For example, Mariah S., from Chicago, **adds up** everything she's spent at the end of the month. T
4. After Mariah **worked out** a budget, she changed some of her spending habits. T
5. She used to pay for an expensive gym membership, but now she works out at home. I
6. She also decided to **give up** expensive dinners in order to save money. T
7. Mariah didn't give up and eventually saved enough money to start a business. I
8. She also **paid back** some money her family had loaned her. T

Exercise 3.2 Transitive Phrasal Verbs page 310

2. add up	6. build up
3. work out	7. Pay off
4. Write down	8. bring; up
5. throw away	9. put off

Exercise 3.3 More Transitive Phrasal Verbs

A page 310

2. A: throw away your receipts / throw your receipts away
   B: throw them away
3. A: put off things / put things off
   B: sort them out
4. A: take out a loan / take a loan out
   B: pay it off
5. A: work out a budget / work a budget out
   B: figure it out

B Pair Work page 310

Answers will vary.

4 Avoid Common Mistakes

Editing Task page 311

It is easy to get into debt. Prices are going ^up all the time.

Maybe you have to change jobs and your income decreases.
Maybe you've picked ^up bad habits, like ordering a pizza

instead of cooking. You are using your credit card more and

more. Soon your debt has grown ~~up~~, and it is more than

you can afford. Or maybe you have a loan and you cannot

pay ~~back it~~ ^*it back*. If you do not watch ^*out*, you may find that you

have thousands of dollars of debt. It is hard to know what

to do with debt that has risen ~~up~~. We can help! Our website

is full of financial advice. It points ^*out* the things you must and

must not do when you get into debt.

> Do you have difficulty with your budget? Read our <u>Budget Guide</u>.
> It will help you figure ~~out it~~ ^*it out*.

> Do you want to get married? Before you do, find ^*out* how your partner feels about money. Do you have different priorities? Read our <u>Money and Relationships Guide</u> and discuss it.

5 Grammar for Writing

Using Transitive and Intransitive Phrasal Verbs

Pre-writing Task

1 page 312

Possible answer: The writer suggests loaning your teen money.

2 page 313

Teenagers have a lot of problems with money. They can easily spend money, but they often do not know how to save

it. Teaching teenagers about money is important, and there are many different ways to do this. One way is to loan your teen money. Imagine your teenage son wants a new cell phone, but he does not have enough money. You can loan him the money and then, each month, your teen can <u>pay</u> you <u>back</u> a percentage of the loan. <u>Sit down</u> with him and <u>work out</u> a realistic amount of time for him to <u>pay</u> the loan <u>back</u>. Then, have your teen <u>figure out</u> exactly how much to give you each month. Do not forget to <u>write</u> the loan agreement <u>down</u> on a piece of paper or in a notebook. In addition, make sure your teen <u>pays back</u> all the money and <u>does not give up</u>. This is a good way for your teen to <u>find out</u> the value of money and possessions. This is a lesson that will last a lifetime.

Transitive phrasal verbs: pay back, work out, pay back, figure out, write down, pays back, find out
Intransitive phrasal verbs: Sit down, does not give up
Objects of transitive phrasal verbs: you, a realistic amount of time, the loan, exactly how much, the loan agreement, all the money, the value

Writing Task

1 Write page 313

Answers will vary.

2 Self-Edit page 313

Answers will vary.

26 Comparatives
We Are All Different

1 Grammar in the Real World

A page 314

Answers will vary.

B Comprehension Check page 315

1. c   2. d   3. a   4. b

C Notice page 315

1. bigger; stronger; than
2. more; adventurous; more; creative; than
Similar: they both show how two things are different
Different: "more" is used before two of the adjectives, the ending -er is used with two of the adjectives

2 Comparative Adjectives and Adverbs
Exercise 2.1 Comparative Forms pages 317–318

2. better than
3. younger
4. worse
5. better
6. more quickly
7. longer
8. more intelligent
9. earlier
10. bigger
11. smaller

Exercise 2.2 More Comparative Forms

A page 318

2. older
3. taller than
4. heavier than
5. less hardworking than
6. harder
7. more conservative
8. more athletic than
9. less friendly than
10. better than

B page 319

Answers will vary.

Exercise 2.3 Comparatives with *Be* and *Do*

A page 319

Possible answers:

2. Louisa is more creative than Sarah is.
3. Sarah lives farther from school than Louisa does.
4. Louisa is better at writing than Sarah is.
5. Sarah learns more quickly than Louisa does.
6. Louisa is quieter than Sarah is.

B page 319

When you cross out *be* or *do*, the meaning is still clear.

C Pair Work page 319

Answers will vary.

Exercise 2.4 More Comparative Practice

A page 320

Answers will vary.

B Group Work page 320

Answers will vary.

3 Comparisons with As . . . As

Exercise 3.1 Forming (*Not*) As . . . As Sentences

A pages 322–323

2. aren't / are not as good as
3. aren't / are not as confident as
4. don't / do not solve problems as easily as
5. aren't / are not as big as
6. do as well as
7. is as hard as
8. are as likely as
9. aren't / are not as aggressive as boys
10. don't / do not get angry as quickly as men
11. can't / cannot throw objects as far as men

B Pair Work page 323

Answers will vary.

Exercise 3.2 Using *As . . . As*

A Pair Work page 323

Answers will vary.

B Group Work page 323

Answers will vary.

Exercise 3.3 Using (*Not*) As . . . As

A Over to You page 324

Answers will vary.

B Pair Work page 324

Answers will vary.

4 Avoid Common Mistakes

Editing Task page 325

I think I have changed in three important ways since high school. First, I have a ~~more~~ kinder personality now. I used to be less patient ~~that~~ *than* I am now, especially with my grandparents. I have spent a lot of time with my grandparents in the last three years, and I have learned to be more patient with them and to understand them ~~more~~ better. I can see that getting old can be ~~more~~ difficult, so I try to help my grandparents as often *as* I can.

Second, I did not use to be as serious *as* I am now about my education. I now realize that I need to study as much *as* possible so I can get a diploma in engineering. Five years ago, I was very ~~younger~~ *young* and did not study a lot. Now I'm studying ~~more~~ harder than I did then, and I do not skip classes as much *as* I did in high school.

Finally, I worry less ~~that~~ *than* I did because I have goals now. I know what I want and where I am going. In general, I have grown up and become ~~more~~ clearer about who I am and what I want out of life. I believe I am a better person ~~that~~ *than* I used to be.

5 Grammar for Writing
Using Comparatives with Adjectives and Adverbs
Pre-writing Task
1 page 326

Possible answer:

The writer's parents were not as strict as his/her friends' parents. They also didn't punish their children as much as other parents did.

2 page 326

Everyone has strong ideas about the right and wrong ways to take care of children. Some parents watch their children (more closely) than others – some are stricter, while others are more lenient. My parents always gave my brother and me a lot of freedom. They were not as strict as our friends' parents. They wanted us to learn to make our own decisions about things. Most of my friends' parents were stricter with their children, and the parents made the decisions for them. Our friends were not allowed to stay out (as late as) we were, for example. Also, when our friends' grades were not as good as they could be, they were punished. When our grades were not good, our parents talked to us about how to do (better) in school. In my opinion, this was more effective. I think my brother and I matured (faster than) some of our friends. I also think some of our friends are less confident about themselves and their decisions than we are. There are many different ways to take care of children, and I feel lucky that my parents raised us the way they did.

Verbs the adverbs compare: watch, stay out, do, matured
Nouns the adjectives compare: parents, grades, this (parents method), friends

Writing Task
1 Write page 327

Answers will vary.

2 Self-Edit page 327

Answers will vary.

27 Superlative Adjectives and Adverbs
The Best and the Worst

1 Grammar in the Real World
A page 328

Answers will vary; Possible answer: People use technology during natural disasters to provide current news and to raise money.

B Comprehension Check page 329

1. Hurricane Katrina happened in 2005.
2. New Orleans was hit the hardest by the hurricane.
3. Craigslist is an online network for free advertising.
4. People used Craigslist to post reports of missing persons and to share news and stories.
5. The Red Cross used social networking sites after the earthquake in Haiti to raise money.

C Notice page 329

Possible answers:

1. No. Another city was not hit harder than New Orleans.
2. No. There didn't seem to be a quicker or more efficient way to get and give information.
3. No. There was no faster worldwide money-raising event.

2 Superlative Adjectives and Adverbs
Exercise 2.1 Superlative Forms page 331

2. (the) hardest	6. (the) most quickly
3. the biggest	7. least damaging
4. the least useful	8. (the) least effectively
5. worst	

Exercise 2.2 More Superlative Forms

A page 332

		Eruption of Mount Vesuvius	Great Chicago Fire
1. bad	*the worst*	☐	☑
2. big	*the biggest*	☐	☑
3. famous	*the most famous*	☑	✓
4. fast	*the fastest*	☐	☑
5. good	*the best*	☐	☑
6. helpful	*the most helpful*	☑	☐
7. important	*the most important*	☑	☐
8. interesting	*the most interesting*	☐	☑
9. popular	*the most popular*	☐	☑

B page 332

1. one of the most famous
2. the most important
3. one of the most helpful
4. the biggest; the worst
5. The most popular
6. the most interesting
7. one of the fastest
8. the best

Exercise 2.3 More Superlative Practice

A page 333

Possible answers:

1. The Westland fire lasted the longest (number of days).
2. The Highside fire lasted the shortest (number of days).
3. The Westland fire was the most damaging.
4. The Highside fire was the least damaging.
5. The Westland fire was the most expensive.
6. The Highside fire was the least expensive.
7. Firefighters arrived the most quickly at the Westland fire.
8. Firefighters arrived the least quickly at the Lakeview fire.

B Pair Work page 333

Answers will vary.

Exercise 2.4 Using Superlatives

A Over to You page 334

Answers will vary.

B Over to You page 334

Answers will vary.

C Pair Work page 334

Answers will vary.

D Group Work page 334

Answers will vary.

3 Avoid Common Mistakes

Editing Task page 335

Hi Miko,

    We had a terrible storm last week. It was the ~~baddest~~ *worst* storm of the decade. It was probably the ~~terrifyingest~~ *most terrifying* experience of my life. The children were home with me. All three of them were scared, but Alexis behaved the ~~wellest~~ *best*. She was the ~~helpfulest~~ *most helpful*. She kept the other children calm. The dog was probably the ~~difficultest~~ *most difficult*! He barked and barked.

    After the storm, we went outside. The damage to our house is the ~~baddest~~ *worst*. ~~Me~~ *My* biggest problem is getting someone to help us fix it. There were some people injured, so rescue workers helped ~~the fastest~~ those people *the fastest*. After that, they started cleaning up ~~the most quickly~~ our neighborhood *the most quickly*. A tree fell on our garage and is still there, so that's ~~us~~ *our* biggest problem right now. We hope someone will move it tomorrow.

Pat

4 Grammar for Writing

Using Superlative Adjectives and Adverbs

Pre-writing Task

1 page 336

Possible answer:

The writer wrote about last year's wildfire. It was so extreme because it was the biggest and it came the closest to the writer's neighborhood.

2 page 336

    There have been a lot of wildfires since we moved to California, but last year's fire was <u>the worst</u> because it was <u>the biggest</u> and it came (the closest) to our neighborhood. It was very hard to put out, and it lasted (the longest) of all the fires in the last few years. We watched the fire begin in the hills behind our neighborhood. At first, it was very small, but it spread quickly. A lot of ash fell on us for days. <u>The thickest</u> ash fell during the first few days of the fire. It looked like thick, white snow. The air was also <u>the smokiest</u> on those days because the winds were blowing (the hardest) then. Those were <u>my family's scariest</u> days and nights. Many people think that lightning is <u>the most common</u> cause of wildfires, but this is not true. People are <u>the biggest</u> cause of wildfires. In fact, the fire behind our neighborhood was caused by people camping in the woods.

Writing Task

1 Write page 337

Answers will vary.

2 Self-Edit page 337

Answers will vary.

28 Gerunds and Infinitives (1)
Managing Time

1 Grammar in the Real World

A pages 338–339

Answers will vary; Possible answer: In some cultures, people see time is linear; in other cultures, people see time as cyclical.

B Comprehension Check page 339

Possible answers:

1. One person is missing and the group has not discussed everything on the agenda.
2. Linear.
3. As a cycle.
4. Get others to help create the agenda and try to be flexible.

C Notice page 339

1. Joe needs (to leave) soon.
2. People from these cultures do not expect (to control) time or events.
3. Joe enjoys (keeping) a schedule.
4. How can Joe avoid (experiencing) problems with multicultural meetings?

The second verbs in sentences 1 and 2 are infinitives, they use the form *to* + verb. The second verbs in sentences 3 and 4 are gerunds, they use the form verb + *-ing*.

2 Verbs Followed by Gerunds or Infinitives

Exercise 2.1 Listening for Gerunds and Infinitives page 341

2. to go
3. to pass
4. to look
5. to arrive
6. to last
7. looking
8. thinking
9. to be
10. looking
11. to have

Exercise 2.2 Gerund or Infinitive? page 342

2. discussing
3. ending
4. to cover
5. continuing
6. combining
7. not doing
8. stopping
9. continuing
10. to arrange
11. you to feel
12. the team to help
13. to write
14. everyone to participate
15. agreeing
16. following it

Exercise 2.3 Using Gerunds and Infinitives

A page 343

Answers will vary.

B Pair Work page 343

Answers will vary.

3 Verbs Followed by Gerunds and Infinitives

Exercise 3.1 Same or Different Meaning?

A pages 344–345

2. My co-workers and I like learning about how different cultures view time. _S_
3. We began to discuss our plans for next year. _S_
4. To manage her time, our colleague Kelly tried buying a calendar. _D_
5. Our boss started accepting that different cultures see time differently. _S_
6. Kelly and I love to have a very long lunch break. _S_
7. Our colleague Bill hates to mix work and social activities. _S_
8. Our co-workers didn't stop to eat lunch until 4:00 p.m. _D_
9. We continued discussing our problems until very late at night. _S_
10. Jill forgot contacting Janet last week. _D_
11. Bo remembered to write and to send the memo. _D_

B Pair Work page 345

Possible answers:

4. In the first sentence, Kelly did not buy the calendar. In the second sentence, Kelly did buy the calendar.
8. In the first sentence, the co-workers ate lunch until 4:00 pm. In the second sentence, the co-workers started lunch at 4:00 pm.
10. In the first sentence, Jill did not call Janet. In the second sentence, Jill didn't remember that she had contacted Janet already.
11. In the first sentence, Bo remembered that he had already written and sent the memo. In the second sentence, Bo stopped to write and send the memo.

Exercise 3.2 *Forget, Remember, Stop,* and *Try* pages 345–346

2. reading
3. to get
4. reading
5. to bookmark
6. to bookmark
7. reading
8. shutting
9. to think

Exercise 3.3 Using Verbs Followed by Gerunds and Infinitives

A Over to You page 346

Answers will vary.

B Pair Work page 346

Answers will vary.

4 Avoid Common Mistakes

Editing Task page 347

Do you keep ~~to look~~ *looking* at the clock when you are bored? Does time seem ~~going~~ *to go* slowly for you? If you expect ~~having~~ *to have* a boring life, you will have a boring life. It is time to make a change! Here are things you can do to avoid ~~to feel~~ *feeling* bored. First, try ^*to* look at the clock less often. Time will go more quickly. Next, use your time differently. Start thinking about things that interest you. Try ^*to* do things that you know will be interesting. If you enjoy ~~to do~~ *doing* an activity, time will pass more quickly. In addition, do things that involve changing your daily habits. For example, try wearing your watch on the other wrist or ~~to brush~~ *brushing* your teeth with the other hand. If your mind is active, time will seem ~~passing~~ *to pass* more quickly.

5 Grammar for Writing
Using Gerunds and Infinitives

Pre-writing Task

1 pages 348–349

Possible answer:

One way to stay organized is to file your papers, or to create a "to do" list.

2 page 349

The expression "There are never enough hours in a day" seems to be true more and more these days. Our lives are filled with lots of tasks. To use your time well, **try organizing** yourself. Learning to do this **involves organizing** both your space and your mind. Organizing your space **involves creating** a way to organize the piles of papers and mail you receive at home, school, and work. **Try dividing** this paper into separate files, for example, have one each for home, work, and school. If you work in an office, you will probably need to organize your papers into several categories. Ones that work very well are "in" and "out" boxes and a "work in process" box. Next, start to organize your mind. Remembering everything you have to do is impossible, so **try creating** a "to do" list. The next step is prioritizing the tasks on the list. Which ones are the most important to finish? When do you expect to finish them? After answering these questions, write the tasks on a calendar. Once you are organized, it is important to stay organized. For example, if you decided to finish your homework in the mornings and go grocery shopping after class, stick to this plan. Also, **focus on finishing** the most important tasks on the calendar. After a week, check how well this new organization is going and make any changes. You will soon find that by managing your time and space, you have saved a lot of time.

Verbs can take gerund or infinitive: try, start. The meaning does not change.

Writing Task

1 Write page 349

Answers will vary.

2 Self-Edit page 349

Answers will vary.

29 Gerunds and Infinitives (2)
Civil Rights

1 Grammar in the Real World

A page 350

Answers will vary; Possible answer: Since the 1960s, discriminating due to age, race, gender, or disabilities have become illegal.

B Comprehension Check page 351

Possible answers:

1. There was discrimination due to age, race, gender, and disabilities.
2. African Americans had to attend separate school and could not buy homes in "white" neighborhoods.
3. Civil rights workers wanted to change the unfair laws.
4. Women and people with disabilities fought for civil rights after Congress passed the Civil Rights Act of 1964.

C Notice page 351

1. Changing   3. to segregate
2. Discriminating   4. to call

Gerunds can also occur as subjects, as seen in sentences 1 and 2. In Sentence 4, "to call" shows a purpose or reason for the action.

2 More About Gerunds
Exercise 2.1 Gerunds as Subjects, After Prepositions, and After *Be*

A pages 352–353

2. refusing   7. supporting
3. doing   8. sending
4. giving   9. pressuring
5. trying   10. getting
6. treating   11. working

Answers will vary.

Exercise 2.2 More Gerunds as Subjects, After Prepositions, and After *Be*

A page 354

3. is involved in starting
4. fighting
5. sitting
6. keep sitting
7. doing
8. succeeds in becoming
9. are involved in marching
10. Not allowing
11. are involved in working

B Group Work page 355

Answers will vary.

3 More About Infinitives

Exercise 3.1 Infinitives After *Be*, to Show Purpose, and with *It* page 356

2. to fight
3. to get
4. to stop
5. to frighten
6. to call
7. to earn

Exercise 3.2 More Infinitives

A pages 356–357

2. to improve
3. to help
4. to focus
5. to be
6. to pay
7. to use
8. to stop
9. to help
10. to get
11. to convince
12. to help
13. to show

B page 358

Possible answers:

1. Being a farm worker in the 1950 was difficult.
2. For example, paying farm workers very low wages was common.
3. Using dangerous pesticides (toxic chemicals) on farm crops was also common.
4. Stopping these things was Chávez's dream.

C Pair Work page 358

Possible answers:

2. He joined a civil rights group in the 1950s to help Mexican Americans register and vote in elections.
3. He gave speeches to focus people's attention on workers' rights.

4. It was difficult to be a farm worker because they were paid very low wages and dangerous pesticides were used on farm crops.
5. In the 1960s, he organized a strike to help farm workers. In the 1980s, Chávez used another strike to convince growers to stop the use of pesticides on grapes.
6. The purpose of César Chávez Day is to show respect for his important work.

D Over to You page 358

Answers will vary.

4 Avoid Common Mistakes

Editing Task page 359

It was more difficult ^to^ be disabled in the United States in the past. It was hard ^to^ do things like enter buildings or cross the street if you were in a wheelchair. In many places, it was impossible ^to^ bring a guide dog into a restaurant. Many people were interested in ~~to help~~ *helping* the disabled. They worked hard ~~for~~ to help people with disabilities. They finally succeeded ~~on~~ *in* passing an important law. It was the Americans with Disabilities Act of 1990. Today, sight-impaired people are not afraid ~~for~~ *of* bringing their dogs into any building. Making streets accessible to people with physical disabilities ~~are~~ *is* another result of the 1990 law. For example, adding gentle slopes to the edges of sidewalks ~~help~~ *helps* the disabled. Now a person in a wheelchair doesn't worry about ~~to get~~ *getting* from one side of the street to the other. Making changes like these ~~are~~ *is* a slow process, but an important one.

5 Grammar for Writing

Using Gerunds and Infinitives

Pre-writing Task

1 page 360

Possible answers:

The paragraph is about working mothers. The problem was that a working mother who took time off to have a baby or take care of a sick child could lose her job. The Family and Medical Leave Act made employers give women 12 weeks off from work to take care of their new babies and offer them a job when they returned to work.

2 page 360

Being a full-time employee and a mother of small children is not easy. What happens when your child gets sick? In the past, you could lose your job for (taking) time off to take care of a sick child or give birth to a baby. Many people struggled to change this situation, and in 1993, the passing of the Family and Medical Leave Act improved things for pregnant women and for families in general in the United States. This law stopped employers from (firing) new mothers. Now, employers have to give employees up to 12 weeks off from work in order to take care of their new babies. In addition, after 12 weeks, employers have to give these women a job again. This law is also good for anyone with a sick child, a sick husband or wife, or even a sick parent.

Writing Task

1 Write page 361

Answers will vary.

2 Self-Edit page 361

Answers will vary.

30 Subject Relative Clauses (Adjective Clauses with Subject Relative Pronouns)
Sleep

1 Grammar in the Real World

A page 362

Answers will vary; Possible answer: Some people only need a few hours of sleep because they have a gene mutation.

B Comprehension Check page 363

Possible answers:

1. A gene mutation might control how much sleep we get.
2. People who do not need a lot of sleep are called short sleepers.
3. Scientists studied a mother and her daughter because they were both short sleepers.
4. The mice that had the gene mutation slept less at night than the mice that didn't have the mutation.

C Notice page 363

1. There are many (people) who need eight or more hours of sleep a night.
2. Researchers recently found a (gene mutation) that might control our sleep.
3. The researchers then created (mice) that had the same hDEC2 gene mutation.
4. The (mice) that did not have the mutation needed extra sleep.

2 Subject Relative Clauses
Exercise 2.1 Subject Relative Clauses
pages 364–365

Many researchers have done studies (that) look at sleep. This article is about a study (that) compares the habits of good sleepers and bad sleepers. A group of scientists (who) specialize in sleep research did the study. First, the scientists studied people (who) sleep well. They learned about the habits (that) might make these people good sleepers. Then the scientists studied people (who) do not sleep well. These short sleepers often have habits (which) are very different from the habits of good sleepers. From this study, the researchers have developed the following tips for people (who) cannot sleep. First, do not drink caffeinated beverages like tea or coffee after noon. In addition, eat dinner at least three hours before going to bed, and, finally, get some exercise every day. These are three habits of good sleepers. If you are a person (who) does not sleep well at night, try to start doing these things. They could help you change your sleep patterns.

Exercise 2.2 *Who, That,* or *Which?*
pages 365–366

1. (people) who
2. (Researchers) who
3. (A study) which
4. (some people) who
5. (People) who
6. (people) who
7. (People) who
8. (Some men and women) who
9. (One idea) which
10. (Another strategy) which

Exercise 2.3 Using Subject Relative Clauses

A page 366

2. who / that; sleeps
3. that / which; give
4. who / that; stays
5. who / that; wakes up
6. who / that; take
7. that / which; helps
8. that / which; help

B Group Work page 366

Answers will vary.

Exercise 2.4 Sentence Combining

A–B page 367

Possible answers:

2. In this study, a sleep expert studied (people) who / that sleep in several different positions.
3. The expert learned many (things) that / which surprised her.
4. (People) who / that sleep in a fetal position tend to be shy and sensitive.
5. (People) who / that sleep on their sides and have their arms at their sides are sociable and relaxed.
6. (People) who / that are quiet and shy sleep on their backs and have their arms at their sides.
7. (People) who / that sleep on their backs and have their arms up near their pillows are friendly and helpful.
8. (People) who / that are easily upset sleep on their stomachs and hug their pillows.

C Group Work page 368

Answers will vary.

3 More About Subject Relative Clauses

Exercise 3.1 Verbs in Subject Relative Clauses pages 368–369

2. who are
3. that is sleeping
4. that lose
5. who needs
6. that sleep
7. that sleep
8. who study
9. that has shown
10. that have shown
11. who were taking

Exercise 3.2 Sentence Combining with *Who, That,* and *Whose*

A pages 369–370

Possible answers:

2. They believe dreams are about certain things which / that represent important ideas or feelings in our lives.
3. People who / that are worried about something dream about losing a tooth.
4. People whose dreams are about flying may have a special wish for freedom.
5. People who / that have a fear of losing control of something dream about falling.
6. People who / that have trouble with friends sometimes dream about a frightening dog.
7. A dream which / that focuses on fire can represent extreme emotions.
8. For example, a person whose room is too hot might also dream of fire.
9. In any case, most people who / that analyze dreams do not see symbols in a simple way.

B Group Work page 371

Answers will vary.

4 Avoid Common Mistakes

Editing Task page 372

Can dreams give us insights into our feelings? Some people who ~~they~~ analyze dreams believe this. There are dream analysts ~~who's~~ *whose* interest is the colors that ~~they~~ are in our dreams. In their opinion, these colors provide clues about our lives. For example, dreams about people ~~which~~ *who / that* are wearing black represent sadness. Dreams ~~who~~ *which / that* have a lot of gray, brown, or tan in them can represent happiness. A dream ~~who's~~ *whose* main color is orange can represent boldness. Many people who ~~analyzes~~ *analyze* dreams think green represents life or new beginnings. On the other hand, there are some people ^ *who / that* do not dream in color. These people dream in black and white. Do you remember the colors that ~~was~~ *were* in your dreams last night? The next time you dream, try to remember the colors. Write down the colors ^ *which / that* appear in your dream, and think about how they made you feel.

5 Grammar for Writing

Using Subject Relative Clauses

Pre-writing Task

1 page 373

Possible answers:

One common cause of sleep problems is worrying. The solution is to make a "to do" list before going to bed.

2 page 373

People (who) have sleep problems need tricks that will help them sleep better. Some of these people have problems getting to sleep, while others have problems falling asleep again after they wake up in the middle of the night. One common cause of sleep problems is worrying. People (whose) problems keep them awake do not always have more problems than other people. Instead, people (whose) worries keep them awake just cannot switch off their minds. Sometimes they think about important problems (which) are bothering them. Sometimes they think about appointments, chores, and meetings (that) are on their schedule for the next day.

One trick (which) can be very helpful is to make a "to do" list before going to sleep every night. This list helps people feel better because they have a plan (that) will help them solve their problems the next day. People (who) do this remove the problems from their minds, and they sleep better.

Writing Task

1 Write page 373

Answers will vary.

2 Self-Edit page 373

Answers will vary.

31 Object Relative Clauses (Adjective Clauses with Object Relative Pronouns)
Viruses

1 Grammar in the Real World

A page 374

Answers will vary; Possible answer: Viruses are easy to get because they are passed in small drops of liquid in the air, because you can get them from a person you touch or stand near, and because viruses can live on surfaces for a few hours.

B Comprehension Check page 375

Possible answers:

1. Viruses cause the common cold and the flu.
2. Viruses spread in small drops of liquid that can live on surfaces or people.
3. They can live from a few minutes to many hours.
4. Wash items an infected person has used, cover your mouth and nose when you cough or sneeze, wash your hands frequently, and stay home if you get sick.

C Notice page 375

1. The common cold and the flu are two well-known (illnesses) that viruses cause.
2. Infected people can pass viruses easily to (others) who they interact with.

2 Object Relative Clauses

Exercise 2.1 Object Relative Clauses

A page 377

In 1918 there was a global flu epidemic. It spread to almost every part of the world. The regions (that) the flu affected ranged from the Arctic to the South Pacific. In addition, the effects (that) it had were devastating. The number of people this flu actually killed ✓ was between 50 and 100 million. However, the number of people (that) the virus infected was around 500 million. This was an epidemic scientists could not control ✓. The virus spread very quickly, and it was very powerful. The people (who) viruses usually affect are very old or very young. However, the people (who) this virus infected were healthy young adults. The 1918 flu was one of the worst natural disasters the world had ever seen ✓.

B Pair Work page 377

Same as **A.**

Exercise 2.2 Combining Sentences
pages 377–378

2. who / that the flu killed
3. who / that the flu usually affects
4. which / that the flu affected
5. which / that scientists could not control
6. which / that scientists do not understand
7. which / that many people fear
8. who / that these strange new viruses affect

Exercise 2.3 Using Object Relative Clauses

A Over to You page 378

2. that / which / ∅; *answers will vary*
3. who / that / ∅; *answers will vary*
4. that / ∅; *answers will vary*
5. *answers will vary;* that / which / ∅
6. *answers will vary;* that / which / ∅
7. *answers will vary;* that / which / ∅

B Pair Work page 379

Answers will vary.

Exercise 2.4 Subject and Object Relative Clauses

A page 379

3. that / which
4. causes
5. who / that / ∅
6. attacks
7. that / which / ∅
8. affects
9. that / which
10. attacks
11. that / which
12. affects
13. who / that
14. have
15. who / that
16. have

B Pair Work   page 379

Possible answers:

Sentences with subject relative pronouns: Sometimes the virus that / which causes the flue isn't serious.; A disease that / which attacks a large number of people and areas is an epidemic.; A lot of people who/that have swine flue have mild symptoms.; Others who/that have the disease have more serious symptoms.

3 More About Object Relative Clauses
Exercise 3.1 Verbs in Object Relative Clauses

A   pages 380–381

2. gives	9. ∅
3. that	10. chose
4. gives	11. that
5. that	12. developed
6. sprays	13. ∅
7. that	14. can do
8. had	

B   page 381

Same as **A.**

C Pair Work   page 381

Answers will vary.

Exercise 3.2 Sentence Combining
pages 381–382

2. whose vaccines we still use
3. which / that / ∅ farm animals often get
4. which / that / ∅ people get from dogs and other animals
5. which / that / ∅ people get from animal bites
6. that / who / whom / ∅ a dog bit
7. that / who / whom / ∅ he cured
8. which / that / ∅ farm animals still get

Exercise 3.3 More Object Relative Clauses

A Over to You   page 382

Possible answers:

2. can do to prevent the common cold is . . .
3. use is . . .
4. worry about the most is . . .
5. worry about the most is . . .

B Pair Work   page 383

Answers will vary.

4 Avoid Common Mistakes
Editing Task   pages 383–384

Are computer viruses similar to human viruses? In some ways, they are. A virus that invades your computer sometimes behaves like a virus that infects your body.

Computer viruses became a serious problem in the 1990s. One of the first types of virus ~~who~~ *that / ∅* computer scientists created was a "worm." A worm is a computer virus that a computer receives ~~it~~ without the user's knowledge. A user ~~who~~ *whose* computer is attacked by a worm may lose data or suffer damage to his or her computer system.

The people ~~which~~ *who / that / ∅* we must blame for the very first worm developed it in 1979. Much like a human virus, the worm of 1979 gradually spread until it became an "epidemic." A virus ~~who~~ *that / ∅* thousands of computers received very rapidly was the famous "Melissa" virus of 1999. Luckily, someone developed a "vaccine" for this virus, and it is no longer the cause of a computer virus epidemic.

However, people continue to create viruses of different kinds. For example, one virus attacks people's electronic address lists and sends e-mails to everyone ~~who~~ *whose* name is on a list. The people who you know ~~them~~ may be surprised when they get an e-mail from you that is really an advertisement!

People ~~who~~ *whose* computers were infected with viruses needed protection, so companies began to produce anti-virus software in the 1990s. Nowadays, a user ~~whom~~ *who* has good anti-virus software doesn't need to worry about a sick computer. However, people create new viruses all the time. Viruses will continue to be a problem, and new computer virus "vaccines" will need to be developed to fight them.

5 Grammar for Writing
Using Object Relative Clauses

Pre-writing Task

1 pages 384–385

Possible answers:

Remedies: Drink plenty of liquids, drink hot ginger and honey tea, use hot pads, and take a lot of flu and cold medications
Prevention techniques: Get enough sleep and stay fit / exercise

2 page 385

Everyone I know has been sick recently. The first symptom (that) everyone gets is a sore throat. The next thing ⌃*that / which* everyone complains about is achy muscles. The things (that) I do to feel better are things (which) my mother and my grandmother taught me. For example, it is a good idea to drink plenty of liquids. For my throat, I drink a hot ginger and honey tea (that) my mother used to make for me. It does not taste very good, and sometimes it burns at first, but after drinking it, my throat always feels better. For aches and pains, I use hot pads (that) I put in the microwave. I also take flu or cold medications (that) I keep in my bathroom.

To avoid getting sick, I try to take care of myself. One of the most important things is getting enough sleep. Most people ⌃*who / that* I know do not sleep enough. The other helpful thing is staying fit. Doctors, scientists, and other people (whose) opinion I respect say that exercise is very important. They say (that) if you do not exercise regularly, you are more likely to get sick.

Writing Task

1 Write page 385

Answers will vary.

2 Self-Edit page 385

Answers will vary.

32 Conjunctions and Adverb Clauses
Special Days

1 Grammar in the Real World

A page 386

Answers will vary; Possible answer: Black Friday is good because it is crucial for the U.S. economy and because retailers offer very low prices. Black Friday is bad because the deals are often not as good as they seem and because shoppers occasionally get into arguments and fistfights.

B Comprehension Check page 387

Possible answers:

1. Retailers can make 18 percent to 40 percent of their yearly sales during the holiday shopping season.
2. Retailers offer very low prices on Black Friday.
3. The deals on Black Friday aren't as good as they seem. People get stressed and angry. There are sometimes fistfights or accidents.
4. You can shop on the weekend or stay home and buy online.

C Notice page 387

1. so   b. 3
2. but   c. 4
3. and   d. 2
4. or

2 Conjunctions

Exercise 2.1 *And, Or, But, So,* and *Yet*
page 389

2. and	8. or
3. and	9. and yet
4. but	10. but
5. and	11. and
6. but not	12. or
7. so	13. and

Exercise 2.2 Repeated Subjects, Verbs, and Prepositions page 390

2. There are good deals and ~~there are~~ special offers.
3. For example, at a lot of stores, I can choose free shipping or ~~I can choose~~ a gift with my purchase.
4. I love the deals but ~~I~~ hate the crowds.
5. People become over-excited and ~~people become~~ aggressive on Black Friday.
6. People push and ~~people~~ fight to get to the deals.
7. I stay home and ~~I~~ shop online, or ~~I~~ order things over the phone.

8. I can buy all of my gifts and ~~I can~~ save money, too.
9. We go shopping as a family and ~~we~~ enjoy our day out together.

Exercise 2.3 Using *And, Or, But,* and *So*

A Pair Work page 390

Answers will vary.

B pages 390–391

	Canada	The United States
1.	1578	1621
2.	Martin Frobisher	English Pilgrims
3.	October	November
4.	Monday	Thursday
5.	Turkey and pumpkin pie	Turkey and pumpkin pie
6.	Saturday, Sunday, or Monday	Thursday
7.	December 26	Black Friday

C page 391

2. but; October
3. Thursday; but
4. the United States and Canada; and
5. and; pumpkin pie
6. but; Saturday, Sunday, or Monday
7. or; Monday
8. but; December 26

Exercise 2.4 More Conjunctions

Group Work page 392

Answers will vary.

3 Adverb Clauses

Exercise 3.1 *Because, Since, Although,* and *Even Though* page 394

2. Although
3. because
4. even though
5. Even though
6. Because
7. because
8. Although

Exercise 3.2 Adverb Clauses page 395

Possible answers:

2. Stores are crowded during the holiday shopping period even though / although some people decide not to give gifts.
   Even though / Although some people decide not to give gifts, stores are crowded during the holiday shopping period.
   Stores are crowded during the holiday shopping period, so some people decide not to give gifts.

3. Although / Even though holiday shopping can be unpleasant and expensive, sometimes people feel like they can't avoid gift giving.
   Sometimes people feel like they can't avoid gift giving even though holiday shopping can be unpleasant and expensive.

4. Gift giving in the right situations can make our relationships with people stronger because it can be a nice reminder of how we feel about other people.
   Because it can be a nice reminder of how we feel about other people, gift giving in the right situations can make our relationships with people stronger.

5. Gift giving varies from culture to culture, so it's a good idea to learn about cultural rules for gift giving.
   It's a good idea to learn about cultural rules for gift giving because gift giving varies from culture to culture.

6. In some cultures, you open a gift as soon as you get it, although / even though you wait until the giver has left in other cultures.

7. A certain color can mean bad luck in some cultures, so people will avoid using the color as a gift wrap.
   Because / Since a certain color can mean bad luck in some cultures, people will avoid using the colora s a gift wrap.

8. Both men and women enjoy gifts, although / even though researchers say that gift giving is more important for females.
   Even though researchers say that gift giving is more important for females, both men and women enjoy gifts.

Exercise 3.3 More Adverb Clauses

A page 396

Possible answers:

2. even though / although / though
3. because / since
4. because / since
5. even though / although / though
6. because / since
7. even though / although / though
8. even though / although / though

B Pair Work page 396

Answers will vary.

4 Avoid Common Mistakes

Editing Task page 397

Possible answers:

    Although
~~Allthough~~ Mother's Day is an old holiday‚ᶺ it may

surprise you to know that Father's Day is a modern holiday.

Some people say the first modern Father's Day was in 1908,
    although
~~althought~~ most people agree it started in 1910. Father's

Day was born in Spokane, Washington, on June 19, 1910. Father's Day was partly the idea of Mrs. Sonora Smart Dodd. Because her father was a single parent and raised six children, she wanted to honor him. Although she suggested her father's June 5 birthday, she did not give the organizers enough time to make arrangements. The holiday moved from June 5 to the third Sunday in June. Father's Day is now a popular holiday. *Although* ~~Althogh~~ people laughed at the idea of Father's Day at first, it gradually became popular.

Because retailers saw an opportunity to increase sales in the 1930s, they started to advertise Father's Day gifts. People then felt that they had to buy gifts for their *fathers. Even* ~~fathers even~~ though they realized this was commercialization, they still bought them. Father's Day is an international holiday. Even though people celebrate it on different dates, it is an important day in many cultures.

5 Grammar for Writing
Using Conjunctions and Adverb Clauses

Pre-writing Task

1 page 398

The writer doesn't like Super Bowl Sunday because he / she doesn't enjoy watching football. The writer likes Halloween because it's a lot of fun answering the door and seeing the children and their costumes.

2 pages 398-399

Super Bowl Sunday is in late January (or) early February. On that day, two football teams play to see which team is the best team in the country. It is not a national holiday, (yet) most people think of it as a holiday. People gather together in living rooms (or) restaurants to watch the game together. The game lasts for several hours. People eat a lot of burgers, hot dogs, pizza, potato chips, nacho chips, (and) other kinds of junk food on that day. I do not enjoy watching football, (so) I always get very bored at Super Bowl Sunday parties.

Halloween is on October 31, (and) it is one of my favorite holidays. Children dress up in costumes (and) walk from house to house asking for candy. It is a lot of fun answering the door (and) seeing the children (and) their costumes. Although this holiday is really a children's holiday, there are always parties for adults to go to. Since most adults wear costumes at these parties, too, it is the one time of year that adults can act like children! Food is important on Halloween, too, (but) who does not like chocolate (and) candy?

Writing Task

1 Write page 398
Answers will vary.

2 Self-Edit page 399
Answers will vary.

Unit Tests with Answer Key

A ready-made Unit Test for each of the 32 units of the Student's Book is provided. The tests are easily scored, using a system found at the beginning of the Answer Key. Each test is available in both pdf and Microsoft Word formats.

Instructional PowerPoint® Presentations

The PowerPoint® presentations offer unit-specific grammar lessons for classroom use. The presentations include interactive versions of the *Grammar Presentations* for each unit.

CD-ROM Terms and Conditions of Use

This is a legal agreement between you ("the customer") and Cambridge University Press ("the publisher") for the *Grammar and Beyond 2 Teacher Support Resource CD-ROM*.

1. **Limited license**
   (a) You are purchasing only the right to use the CD-ROM and are acquiring no rights, express or implied, to the software itself, or the enclosed copy, other than those rights granted in this limited license for educational use only.
   (b) The publisher grants you the license to use one copy of this CD-ROM on your site and to install and use the software on this CD-ROM on a single computer. You may not install the software on this CD-ROM on a single secure network server for access from one site.
   (c) You shall not: (i) copy or authorize copying of the CD-ROM, (ii) translate the CD-ROM, (iii) reverse-engineer, alter, adapt, disassemble, or decompile the CD-ROM, (iv) transfer, sell, lease, lend, profit from, assign, or otherwise convey all or any portion of the CD-ROM, or (v) operate the CD-ROM from a mainframe system.

2. **Copyright**
   All titles and material contained within the CD-ROM are protected by copyright and all other applicable intellectual property laws, and international treaties. Therefore, you may not copy the CD-ROM. You may not alter, remove, or destroy any copyright notice or other material placed on or with this CD-ROM.

3. **Liability**
   The CD-ROM is supplied "as-is" with no express guarantee as to its suitability. To the extent permitted by applicable law, the publisher is not liable for costs of procurement of substitute products, damages, or losses of any kind whatsoever resulting from the use of this product, or errors or faults in the CD-ROM, and in every case the publisher's liability shall be limited to the suggested list price or the amount actually paid by the customer for the product, whichever is lower.

4. **Termination**
   Without prejudice to any other rights, the publisher may terminate this license if you fail to comply with the terms and conditions of the license. In such event, you must destroy all copies of the CD-ROM.

5. **Governing law**
   This agreement is governed by the laws of England, without regard to its conflict of laws provision, and each party irrevocably submits to the exclusive jurisdiction of the courts of England. The parties disclaim the application of the United Nations Convention on the International Sale of Goods.